Best Editorial Cartoons of the Year

BUSHWACKER

HARVELL
GREENVILLE PIEDMONT © '90

ROGER HARVELL
Courtesy Greenville News-Piedmont

BEST EDITORIAL CARTOONS OF THE YEAR

1991 EDITION

Edited by
CHARLES BROOKS

PELICAN PUBLISHING COMPANY

Gretna 1991

First printing, April 1991
Second printing, November 1991

Library of Congress Serial Catalog Data

Best editorial cartoons. 1972-
    Gretna [La.] Pelican Pub. Co.
    v. 29 cm. annual-
"A pictorial history of the year."

    1. United States- Politics and government –
1969 – Caricatures and Cartoons – Periodicals.
E839.5.B45   320.9'7309240207   73-643645
ISSN 0091-2220   MARC-S

Manufactured in the United States of America
Published by Pelican Publishing Company, Inc.
1101 Monroe Street, Gretna, Louisiana 70053

Contents

Award-Winning Cartoons

1990 PULITZER PRIZE

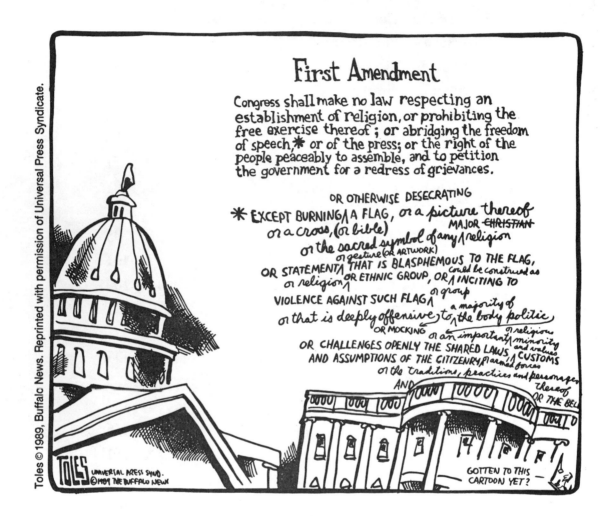

TOM TOLES

Editorial Cartoonist
Buffalo News

Native of Hamburg, New York; graduated from the University of Buffalo, 1973; began career as an editorial cartoonist for the Buffalo *Courier-Express*, 1980; currently editorial cartoonist for the Buffalo *News*; winner of Menken Award for cartooning, 1990; cartoons are syndicated to more than 150 newspapers by Universal Press Syndicate.

1989 NATIONAL SOCIETY OF PROFESSIONAL JOURNALISTS AWARD

(Selected in 1990)

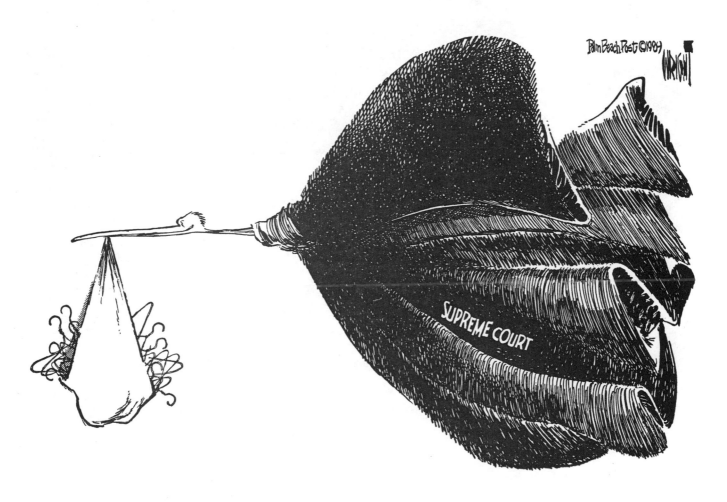

DON WRIGHT
Editorial Cartoonist
Palm Beach Post

Winner of Pulitzer Prize for cartooning, 1966, 1980; winner of the Overseas Press Club Award five times; two-time winner of the Robert F. Kennedy Memorial Journalism Award; winner of the National Headliner Award, 1980. Cartoonist for the Palm Beach, Florida, *Post*, he has published two books, and his work is permanently displayed at Syracuse University. His animated works are distributed by Newsweek Broadcasting Service.

ROBERT ARIAIL

Editorial Cartoonist
The State

Native of Columbia, South Carolina; graduated from the University of South Carolina; named distinguished alumnus of University of South Carolina College of Applied Professional Sciences, 1985; editorial cartoonist for *The State*, the largest newspaper in South Carolina, 1984 to present; created and drew cartoons for motion picture *Don't Tell Her It's Me*.

1990 FISCHETTI AWARD

JEFF STAHLER
Editorial Cartoonist
Cincinnati Post

Native of Bellefontaine, Ohio; graduate of the Columbus College of Art and Design, Columbus, Ohio, 1977; editorial cartoonist for the Columbus *Citizen-Journal*, 1984-85; nationally syndicated by the Newspaper Enterprise Association.

1990 OVERSEAS PRESS CLUB AWARD

JIM MORIN
Editorial Cartoonist
Miami Herald

Born in Washington, D.C.; graduated from Syracuse University, 1976; editorial cartoonist for the Beaumont, Texas, *Enterprise* and *Journal*, 1976-77, the Richmond *Times-Dispatch*, 1977-78, and the Miami *Herald*, 1978 to the present; previously won the Overseas Press Club Award in 1979 and OPC Citation of Excellence in 1983; author of two books, *Famous Cats* (1982) and *Jim Morin's Field Guide to Birds* (1985); cartoons syndicated internationally by King Features Syndicate.

1989 NATIONAL NEWSPAPER AWARD/CANADA
(Selected in 1990)

CAMERON CARDOW
Editorial Cartoonist
Regina Leader-Post

Born in Ottawa, Canada; studied animation and art in Toronto; began career as illustrator for the *Ottawa Citizen*, 1984; editorial cartoonist for the *Regina Post-Leader*, 1987 to the present; cartoons appear in daily newspapers throughout Canada; works have been published in *The Editorial Cartoons of Cam*.

Best Editorial Cartoons of the Year

MIDEAST SCORE BOARD

IRAQ	IRAN	SYRIA	JORDAN
~~GOOD GUY~~	~~BAD GUY~~	~~BAD GUY~~	~~GOOD GUY~~
BAD GUY	~~GOOD GUY~~	GOOD GUY	~~BAD GUY~~
	BAD GUY		~~GOOD GUY~~
			BAD GUY

Persian Gulf Conflict

On August 2, 1990, armed forces of Iraq invaded neighboring Kuwait and occupied the small oil-rich country. The main invasion force of more than 100,000 troops then raced to the border of Saudi Arabia, threatening more than two-thirds of Mideast oil production. The U.S. and the United Nations Security Council condemned the action, and hundreds of thousands of American and Allied troops were rushed to the Saudi desert.

Iraqi President Saddam Hussein built his occupying force to more than half a million troops by year's end and announced the annexation of Kuwait. Iraq held thousands of hostages, including foreign workers from scores of other countries, and threatened to use them as "human shields" in the event of a U.S. attack. As a result of the invasion, oil prices skyrocketed and a virtual worldwide embargo was instituted on goods to or from Iraq.

At year's end, Iraqi forces remained poised in defensive positions on the Kuwait-Saudi Arabia border. Diplomatic talks involving numerous world leaders failed to defuse the crisis, and the United Nations gave Hussein a January 15 deadline to pull out of Kuwait or risk a devastating war. Iraq ignored the deadline, and one day later Allied forces initiated an intensive bombing campaign against Iraq.

JIM TODD
Courtesy Southam Syndicate

JEFF MACNELLY
Courtesy Chicago Tribune

JIM BORGMAN
Courtesy Cincinnati Enquirer

CRAIG MACINTOSH
Courtesy Minneapolis Star-Tribune

JOHN DEERING
Courtesy Arkansas Democrat

BOB GORRELL
Courtesy Richmond News-Leader

AISLIN
Courtesy Montreal Gazette

ROB ROGERS
Courtesy Pittsburgh Press

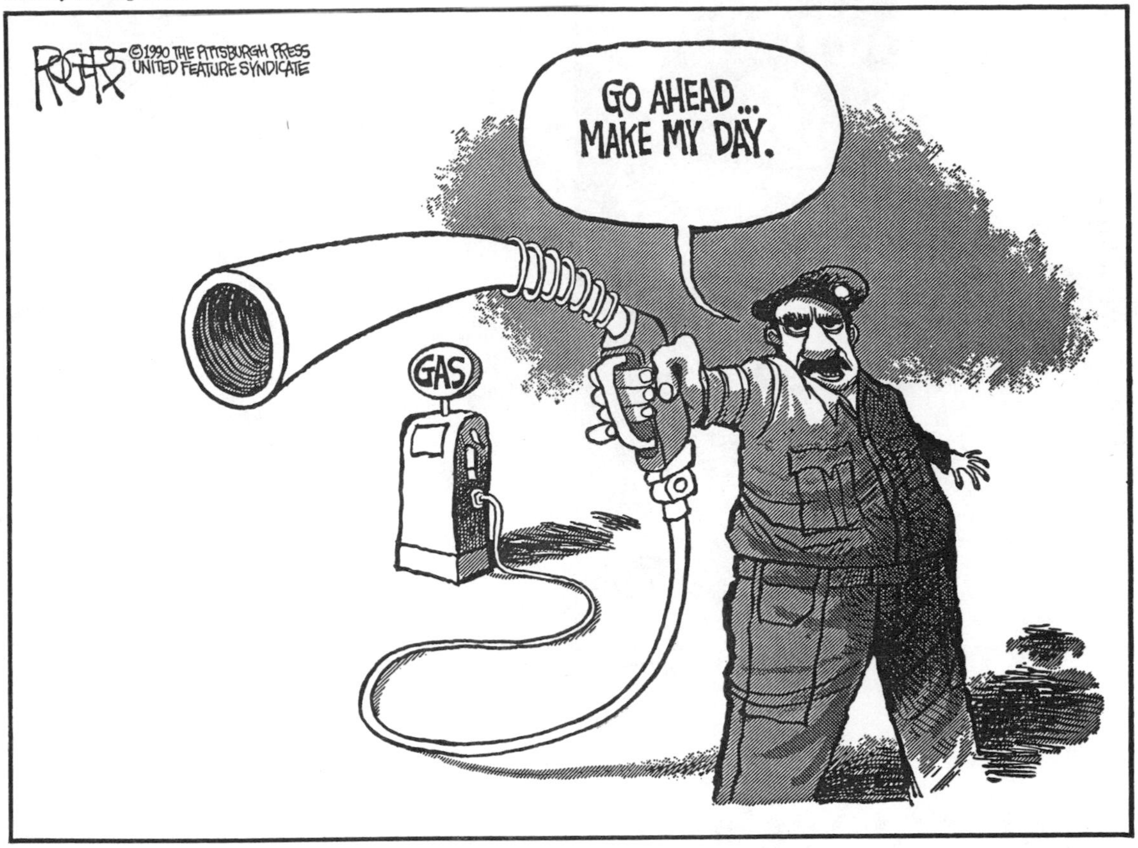
ROGERS ©1990 THE PITTSBURGH PRESS UNITED FEATURE SYNDICATE
GO AHEAD... MAKE MY DAY.
GAS

JOE HELLER
Courtesy Green Bay Press-Gazette

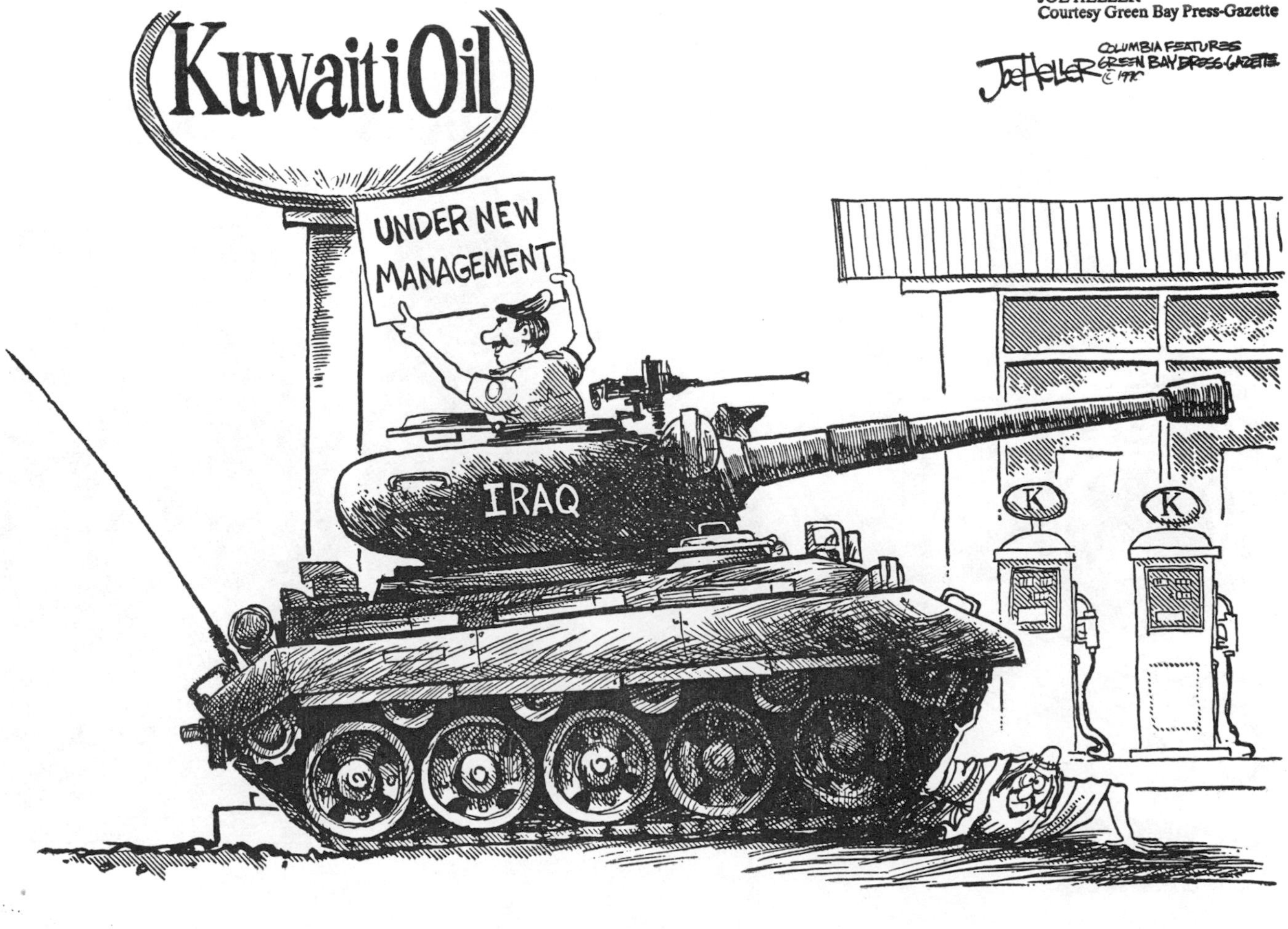
Kuwaiti Oil
UNDER NEW MANAGEMENT
IRAQ
K
K
JOE HELLER COLUMBIA FEATURES GREEN BAY PRESS-GAZETTE

JACK MCLEOD
Courtesy Army Times

JIM LANGE
Courtesy Daily Oklahoman

ANN CLEAVES
Courtesy La Prensa San Diego

ALL WE ARE SAYING....IS GIVE WAR A CHANCE....

MIKE PETERS
Courtesy Dayton Daily News

JIM MORIN
Courtesy Miami Herald

LEN BORO
Courtesy Phoenix Gazette

SDI (SADDAM DEFENSE INITIATIVE)

JORDAN'S KING HUSSEIN... BETWEEN IRAQ AND A HARD PLACE

PAUL SZEP
Courtesy Boston Globe

ART HENRIKSON
Courtesy Des Plaines Daily Herald

JIM BERTRAM
Courtesy St. Cloud Times

GENE BASSET
Courtesy Atlanta Journal

DAVID HORSEY
Courtesy Seattle Post-Intelligencer

©1990 SEATTLE POST-INTELLIGENCER
NORTH AMERICA SYNDICATE

STEVE LINDSTROM
Courtesy Duluth News-Tribune

TOM DARCY
Courtesy Newsday

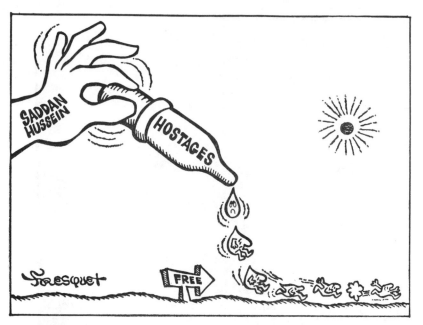

LAZARO FRESQUET
Courtesy El Nuevo Herald

FRANK CAMMUSO
Courtesy Syracuse Herald-Journal

TOM TOLES
Courtesy Buffalo News

JERRY BARNETT
Courtesy Indianapolis News

"As allies, we felt we had to share the burden of America's military commitment.
Here's a $600 rebate coupon for your next Toyota or BMW."

THE THIEF OF BAGHDAD IN HIS HIDEOUT

INDEPENDENCE!
FREEDOM!
DEMOCRACY!
CHEAP OIL!
KIRK©90

KIRK ANDERSON
Courtesy Madison Capital Times

CHUCK AYERS
Courtesy Akron Beacon-Journal

©1990 AKRON BEACON JOURNAL
CHUCK AYERS
KUWAIT
★★★
INVASION
BUILDUP
WAR

VULTURES?
DEMOCRATIC PRESIDENTIAL HOPEFULS...
OPERATION DESERT SHIELD
Omaha World-Herald
JEFF KOTERBA

JEFF KOTERBA
Courtesy Omaha World-Herald

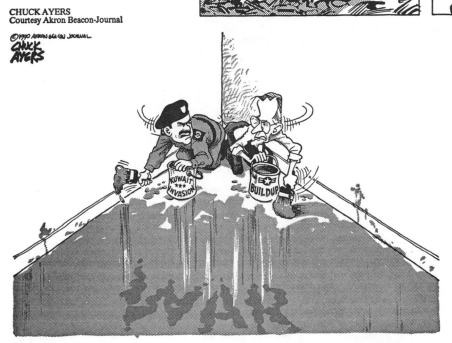

TIM HARTMAN
Courtesy Valley News Dispatch (Pa.)

The Bush Administration

"Read my lips; no new taxes!" insisted George Bush while campaigning for president. But in 1990 he reversed that stand and marched in step with Democrats to raise taxes in an attempt to reduce the budget deficit. He also sacrificed another campaign pledge – his insistence on a cut in the capital gains tax. Bush first flip-flopped on the tax plans as Congress wrestled with them, but finally backed the final agreement. Many Republicans were incensed that their leader had abandoned his oft-repeated pledge, and there was considerable evidence that the GOP suffered in the November elections because of it.

In contrast to his debacle on the budget, the president received high marks across the board for his initial handling of Iraq's invasion of Kuwait. He led a worldwide campaign to isolate and embargo Iraq and succeeded in obtaining the backing of most of the world's leaders. The embargo was enforced by an armada of U.S. and other nations' ships, and a massive buildup of multinational troops took place in Saudi Arabia. At year's end, some 400,000 American troops, along with some 250,000 troops from other nations, stood poised in the Arabian desert awaiting orders to retake Kuwait. The war began January 16.

President Bush extended for an additional year most-favored nation status to China over the objections of Congress and diluted the sanctions his administration and Congress had imposed following the Tiananmen Square massacre in 1989. Few Americans seemed to favor either.

KENNETH CATALINO
Courtesy Anchorage Times

GEORGE DANBY
Courtesy Bangor Daily News

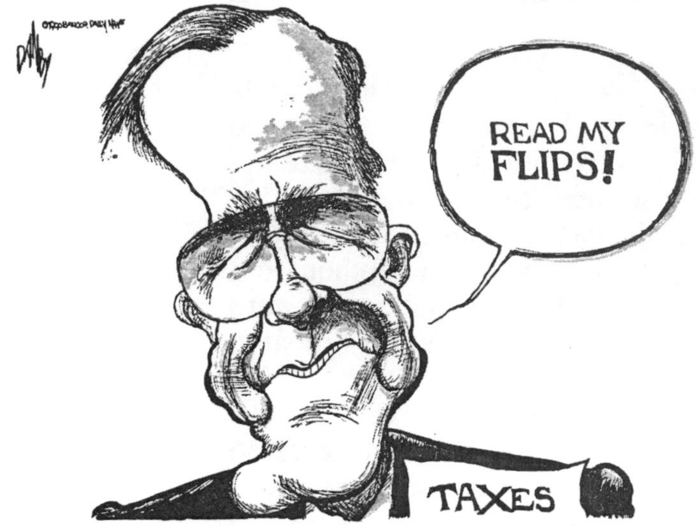
READ MY FLIPS!
TAXES

RANDY WICKS
Courtesy The Signal (Calif.)

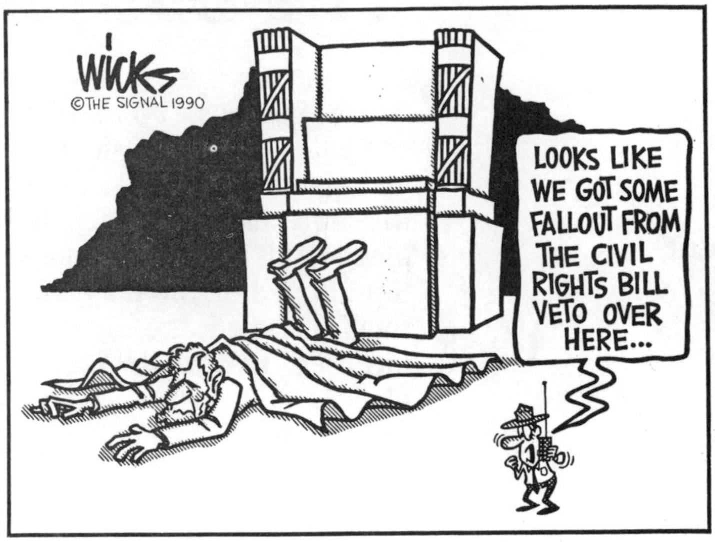
WICKS
©THE SIGNAL 1990
LOOKS LIKE WE GOT SOME FALLOUT FROM THE CIVIL RIGHTS BILL VETO OVER HERE...

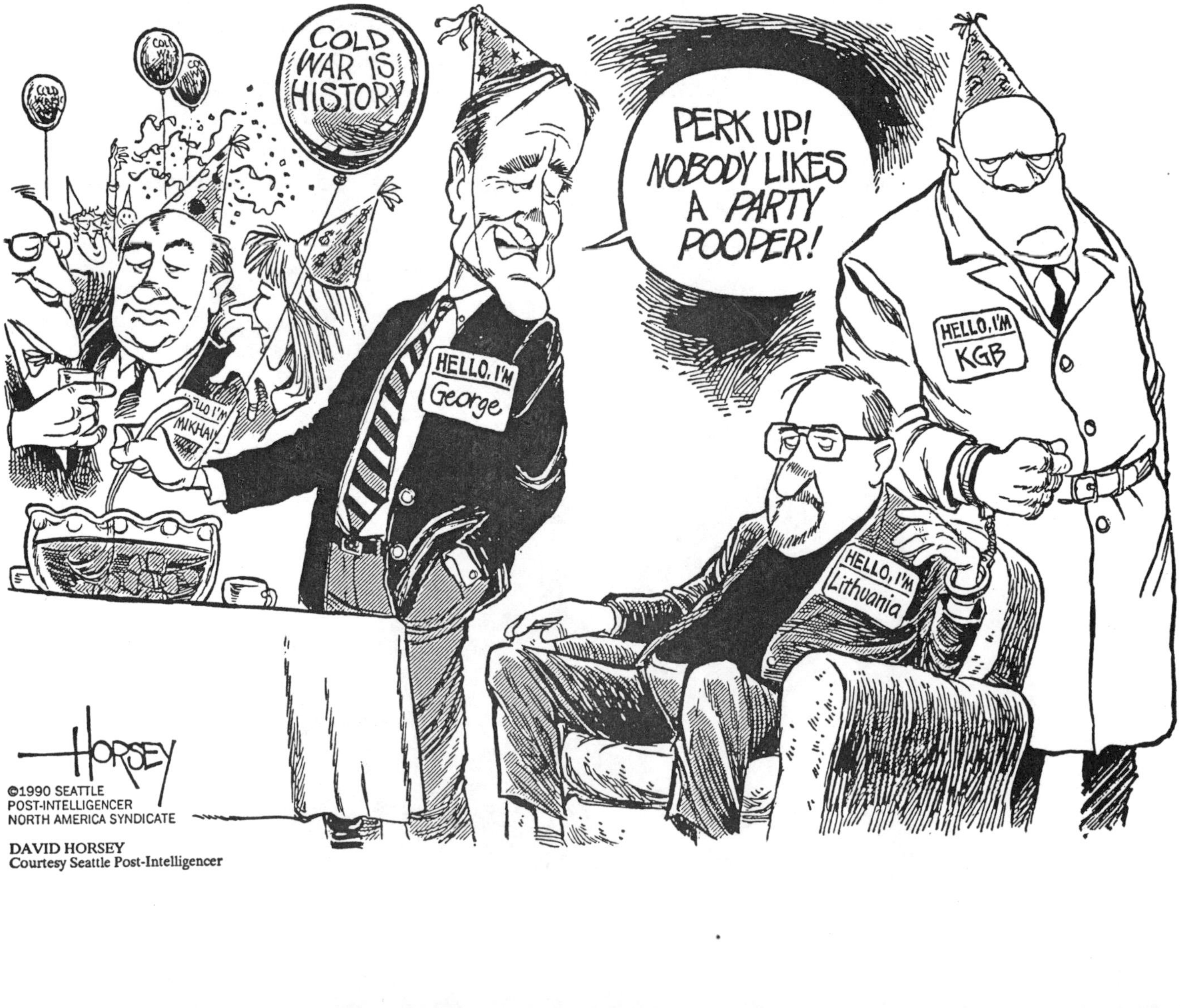
COLD WAR IS HISTORY
PERK UP! NOBODY LIKES A PARTY POOPER!
HELLO, I'M George
HELLO I'M MIKHAIL
HELLO, I'M KGB
HELLO, I'M Lithuania
HORSEY
©1990 SEATTLE POST-INTELLIGENCER NORTH AMERICA SYNDICATE

DAVID HORSEY
Courtesy Seattle Post-Intelligencer

"THAT'S GOOD...HANG IT RIGHT THERE!"

GARY VARVEL
Courtesy Indianapolis News

TOM ENGELHARDT
Courtesy St. Louis Post-Dispatch

'Turn Your Hose Over Here —
My Friend Needs His Pool Filled'

JOHN SPENCER
Courtesy Philadelphia Business Journal

DANA SUMMERS
Courtesy Orlando Sentinel

CHUCK AYERS
Courtesy Akron Beacon-Journal

KEVIN SIERS
Courtesy Charlotte Observer

WALT HANDELSMAN
Courtesy New Orleans Times-Picayune

The Soviet Union

Efforts at political reform continued in the Soviet Union during 1990, but economic deterioration across the country threatened to undermine Mikhail Gorbachev's *perestroika*. With the election of numerous reform-minded candidates, hundreds of small political parties and organizations appeared and began issuing demands for meaningful change. Some urged a retreat to a tsarist-type government while others wanted to institute more democratic reforms.

Boris Yeltsin was elected head of the Russian Republic, the largest state in the Soviet Union, thus making him the second-ranking elected official in the country. Yeltsin called for a more decentralized government, while Gorbachev insisted that the central government must remain supreme. Ethnic violence and calls for secession reached the crisis stage during the year, and work stoppages shook several Soviet republics. The three Baltic republics, particularly—Estonia, Latvia, and Lithuania—which had been forcibly annexed to the Soviet Union in 1940, clamored for independence.

The Soviet economy was in shambles, with shortages of food and consumer goods not experienced since World War II. Hoarding became commonplace as the government moved to dismantle its central planning system, but there was no system to take its place. Even though 1990 was a bumper year for Soviet agriculture, transportation to market was so inefficient that crops rotted in the fields.

DICK LOCHER
Courtesy Chicago Tribune

BRUCE PLANTE
Courtesy Chattanooga Times

ROBERT ARIAIL
Courtesy Columbia State (S.C.)

ROGER HARVELL
Courtesy Greenville News-Piedmont

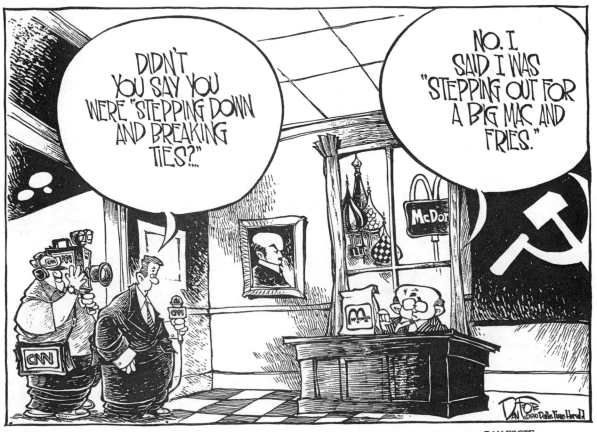

DAN FOOTE
Courtesy Dallas Times-Herald

ROD WARREN
Courtesy Bakersfield Californian

FRED CURATOLO
Courtesy Edmonton Sun

GLENN MCCOY
Courtesy Belleville News-Democrat (Ill.)

PAUL SZEP
Courtesy Boston Globe

AT THE SUMMIT

WILLIAM COSTELLO
Courtesy Lowell Sun

SPYDER WEBB
Courtesy Associated Features

TRUE LOVE IN MOSCOW

JEFF DANZIGER
Courtesy Christian Science Monitor

JERRY FEARING
Courtesy St. Paul Pioneer Press-Dispatch

CAMERON CARDOW
Courtesy Regina Leader-Post

BRUCE MACKINNON
Courtesy Halifax Herald

DICK WALLMEYER
Courtesy Long Beach Press-Telegram

Wallmeyer

1990, PRESS-TELEGRAM

NOBEL LAUREATE

CAUTION
WORKMAN
ABOVE
M. GORBACHEV
WRECKING CO.

ENGELHARDT
© 1990 ST. LOUIS POST-DISPATCH

TOM ENGELHARDT
Courtesy St. Louis Post-Dispatch

BETSY ROSSKY

RAY OSRIN
Courtesy Cleveland Plain Dealer

BRUCE MACKINNON
Courtesy Halifax Herald

NOAH BEE
Courtesy Jewish Telegraphic Agency

LARRY WRIGHT
Courtesy Detroit News

DENNIS PRICHARD
Courtesy Ottawa Citizen

44

DER
THE GREENVILLE NEWS©

LAMBERT DER
Courtesy Greenville News-Piedmont

GARY MARKSTEIN
Courtesy Tribune Newspapers

"I GOTTA HAND IT TO GORBACHEV. HE HAS ACHIEVED A 'GREATER OPENNESS!'"

FRED CURATOLO
Courtesy Edmonton Sun

German Reunification

Massive demonstrations demanding freedom swept across East Germany in late 1989, and tens of thousands of citizens fled tyranny to the West. This latter-day exodus forced the East German authorities to open the Berlin Wall to all who wished to cross, a move that both stunned and delighted the world. It was apparent that East German socialism had failed economically, and thousands of citizens poured through the Wall to West Berlin to shop for coveted goods and to embrace friends and relatives they had not seen for almost three decades.

East German demonstrators began carrying banners proclaiming that "We Are ONE People," and in January 1990 Mikhail Gorbachev declared that he did not oppose "the reunification of the Germans." On October 3, 1990, forty-five years after Germany was divided following World War II, socialist East Germany and democratic West Germany were once again united in a single nation. West German President Richard von Weizsacker was named president of the new Germany, and the German flag was raised in front of the Reichstag Building in Berlin.

Gorbachev agreed that a united Germany was free to become a member of the North Atlantic Treaty Alliance (NATO) if it would reduce its military force and provide the Soviets with large-scale economic, managerial, and technological assistance.

The East Germans clearly required massive economic aid also, and both parts of the new Germany seemed willing to do whatever had to be done to make their nation a permanent entity.

MIKE LUCKOVICH
Courtesy Atlanta Constitution

MIKE Luckovich ATLANTA CONSTITUTION

JERRY HOLBERT
Courtesy Boston Herald

SCOTT STANTIS
Courtesy Arizona Republic

STEVE MCBRIDE
Courtesy Independence (Kan.) Daily Reporter

DRAPER HILL
Courtesy Detroit News

AISLIN
Courtesy Montreal Gazette

DENNIS PRICHARD
Courtesy Ottawa Citizen

S&L Scandal

Financial analysts concluded in 1990 that the savings and loan crisis that has rocked the U.S. economy was caused by three major factors: deregulation, industry abuses, and changing economic conditions. As more and more S&L institutions failed across the country, estimates of the costs to taxpayers rose to as much as $500 billion.

The largest failures of the thrifts occurred in Texas, California, and Arizona as the oil industry and real estate market slumped.

Taxpayers, of course, will ultimately have to pay the gigantic bill for the failed S&Ls, and the public has been outraged by estimates that as many as one-ninth of all S&L losses have been the result of outright fraud. Many S&L executives took advantage of relaxed regulations and the boom period of the 1980s to enrich themselves illegally. One of the largest institutions to collapse was Charles Keating's Lincoln Savings and Loan in California, a failure expected to cost more than $2 billion. Hearings were held in Washington to determine whether the "Keating Five," a group of U.S. senators, had intervened improperly in Keating's behalf.

Neil Bush, the son of President Bush, was accused of negligence and conflict of interest while he served as a director of the Denver Silverado Banking, Savings and Loan Association, another failed institution that could cost taxpayers more than $1 billion.

SCOTT STANTIS
Courtesy Arizona Republic

GENE BASSET
Courtesy Atlanta Journal

MIKE SHELTON
Courtesy Orange County Register

THE S+L BAILOUT

' Amateurs!..'

er...HOW MANY S&Ls DID HE SAY WOULD BE INVOLVED IN THIS BAILOUT?

VIC HARVILLE
Courtesy Arkansas Democrat

JIM MORIN
Courtesy Miami Herald

WALT HANDELSMAN
Courtesy New Orleans Times-Picayune

©1990 THE TIMES-PICAYUNE
WALT HANDELSMAN
TRIBUNE MEDIA SERVICES

©1990 THE (TOLEDO) BLADE KIRK

KIRK WALTERS
Courtesy Toledo Blade

S. C. RAWLS
Courtesy NEA

JOHN DEERING
Courtesy Arkansas Democrat

MIKE SMITH
Courtesy Las Vegas Sun

ERIC SMITH
Courtesy Annapolis Capital-Gazette

KENNETH CATALINO
Courtesy Anchorage Times

DOUG BEEKMAN
Courtesy Montpelier Times Argus

Foreign Affairs

Margaret Thatcher resigned as British prime minister on November 22, thus ending eleven and a half years in office, the longest continuous term of any British prime minister this century. Her perceived foot-dragging on the European integration issue apparently had turned the British public against her.

In post-Tiananmen Square China, passive resistance took the place of activism. The Communist party faced a crisis, since its leadership was comprised primarily of men in their seventies and eighties. Industrial workers found themselves caught between inflation and government austerity programs as the gerontocracy struggled to find ways to improve the nation's woeful standard of living.

Nelson Mandela, a South African anti-apartheid leader imprisoned for twenty-seven years, was released in February. He soon made a six-week tour of fourteen nations, and was received as a hero. He was invited to address a joint session of the U.S. Congress, but provoked criticism when he referred to Fidel Castro, Moammar Qaddafi, and Yasir Arafat as "comrades."

Philippine President Corazon Aquino survived numerous coup attempts as economic problems multiplied. An earthquake in Luzon killed 1,600 persons and injured hundreds of others.

A landmark treaty was signed in Paris in November between NATO and the Warsaw Pact countries, significantly cutting back conventional armed forces in Europe. Problems in Cuba mounted as the Soviet Union drastically reduced economic aid to the Castro government.

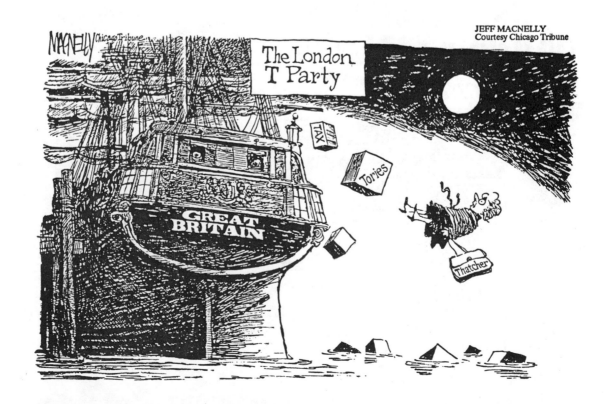

JEFF MACNELLY
Courtesy Chicago Tribune

CHARLES BISSELL
Courtesy The Tennessean

*'SEND NOT TO KNOW FOR WHOM THE CALL COMES –
IT COMES FOR THEE'*

DAVE GRANLUND
Courtesy Middlesex News

THE LIFTING OF MARTIAL LAW

CHINA

©1990 FORT WORTH STAR-TELEGRAM

ETTA HULME
Courtesy Fort Worth Star-Telegram

THE PEOPLE'S REPUBLIC OF CHINA IS MOST PLEASED TO ANNOUNCE THE LIFTING OF MARTIAL LAW.

CLYDE WELLS
Courtesy Augusta Chronicle

Berry's World

NATO

NATO

NATO

NATO

© 1990 by NEA, Inc.

MᶜIVANS
DINOSAURBURGERS

meat grinder

BOB ENGLEHART
Courtesy Hartford Courant

Englehart
THE HARTFORD
COURANT
© 1990 COPLEY NEWS
SERVICE

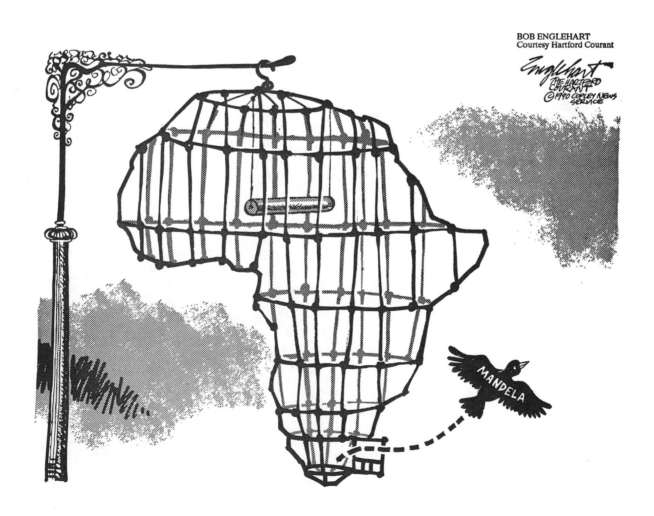

MANDELA

'COUP-RAZON' AQUINO: 'COUP-MANDER-IN-CHIEF"

DANI AGUILA
Courtesy Filipino Reporter

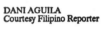

JIM TODD
Courtesy Southam Syndicate

COME 'N GET IT

SPYDER WEBB
Courtesy Associated Features

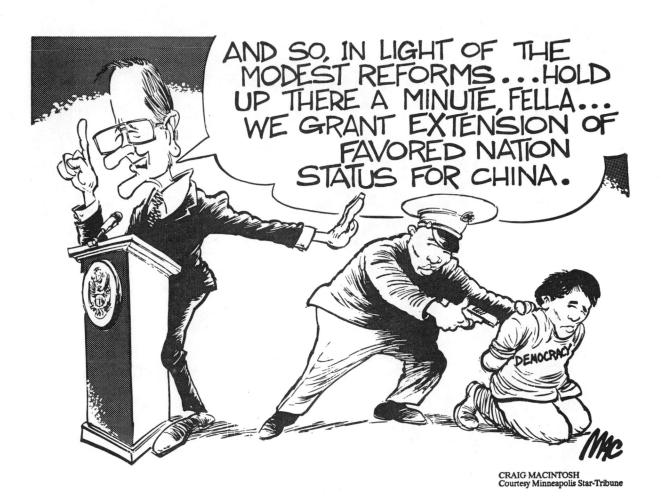

CRAIG MACINTOSH
Courtesy Minneapolis Star-Tribune

BILL SANDERS
Courtesy Milwaukee Journal

DICK WRIGHT
Courtesy Providence Journal-Bulletin

MIKE SMITH
Courtesy Las Vegas Sun

ETTA HULME
Courtesy Fort Worth Star-Telegram

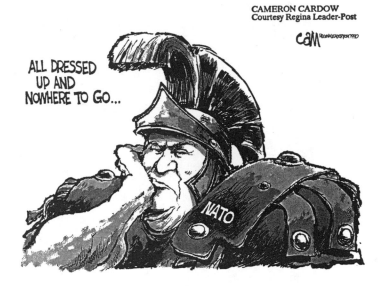

CAMERON CARDOW
Courtesy Regina Leader-Post

DAVE GRANLUND
Courtesy Middlesex News

LARRY WRIGHT
Courtesy Detroit News

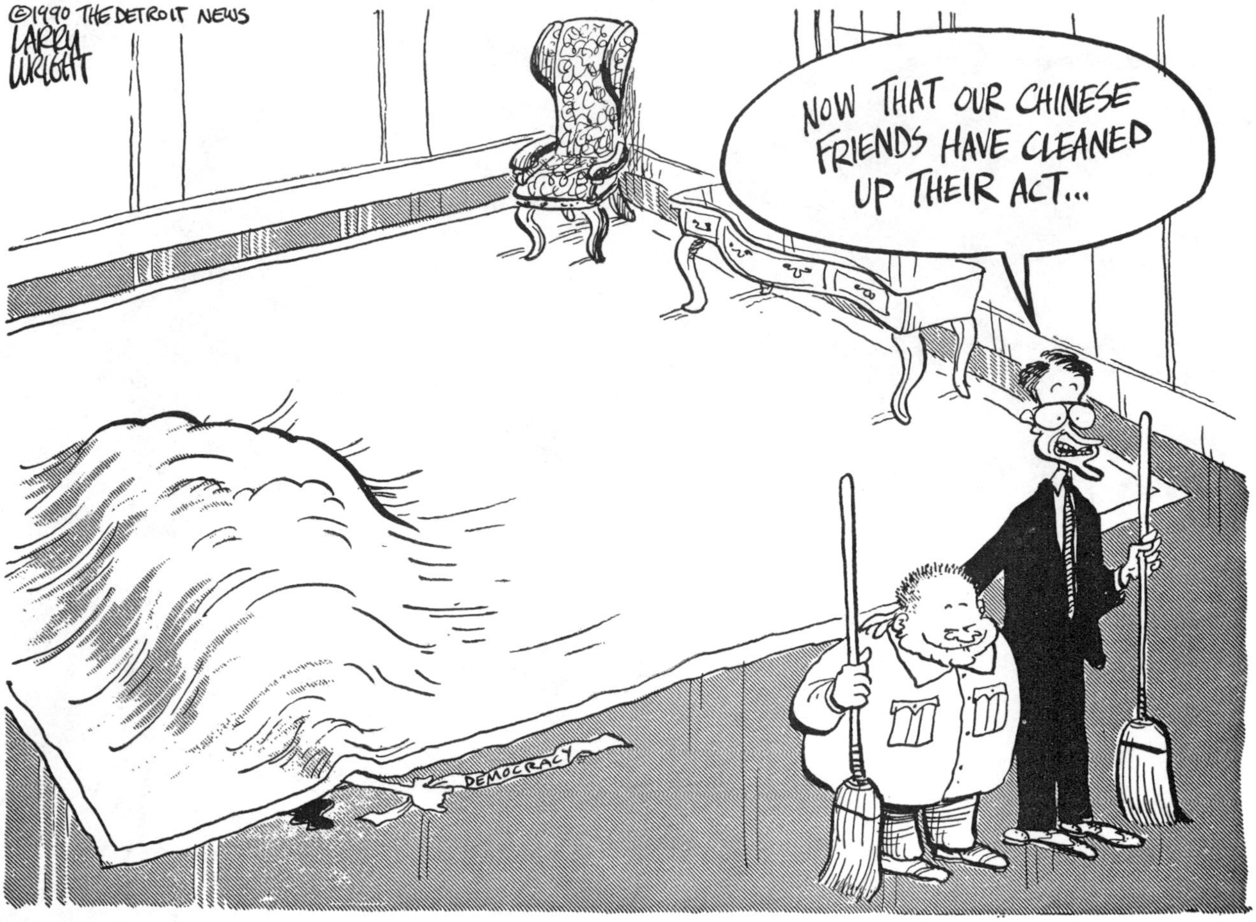
©1990 THE DETROIT NEWS
LARRY WRIGHT
NOW THAT OUR CHINESE FRIENDS HAVE CLEANED UP THEIR ACT...
DEMOCRACY

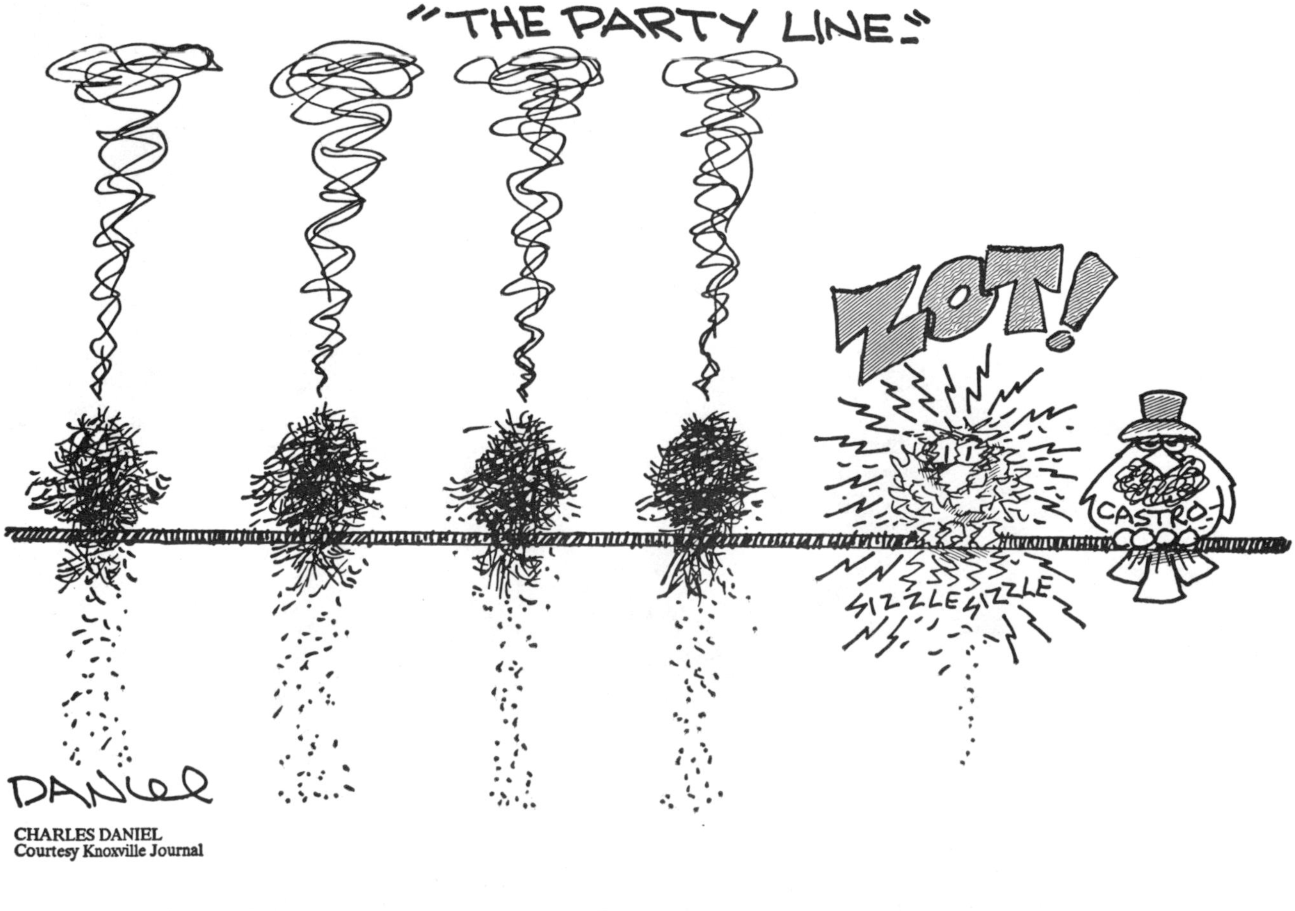
"THE PARTY LINE."
ZOT!
SIZZLE SIZZLE
CASTRO
DANIEL

CHARLES DANIEL
Courtesy Knoxville Journal

CONTRIBUTIONS TO THE WAR ON APARTHEID

TOM GIBB
Courtesy Altoona Mirror

FOUGHT IT. LANGUISHED IN PRISON BECAUSE OF IT. DEVOTED HIS LIFE TO ELIMINATING IT.

LEARNED TO PRONOUNCE IT.

CRAIG MACINTOSH
Courtesy Minneapolis Star-Tribune

BRIAN DUFFY
Courtesy Des Moines Register

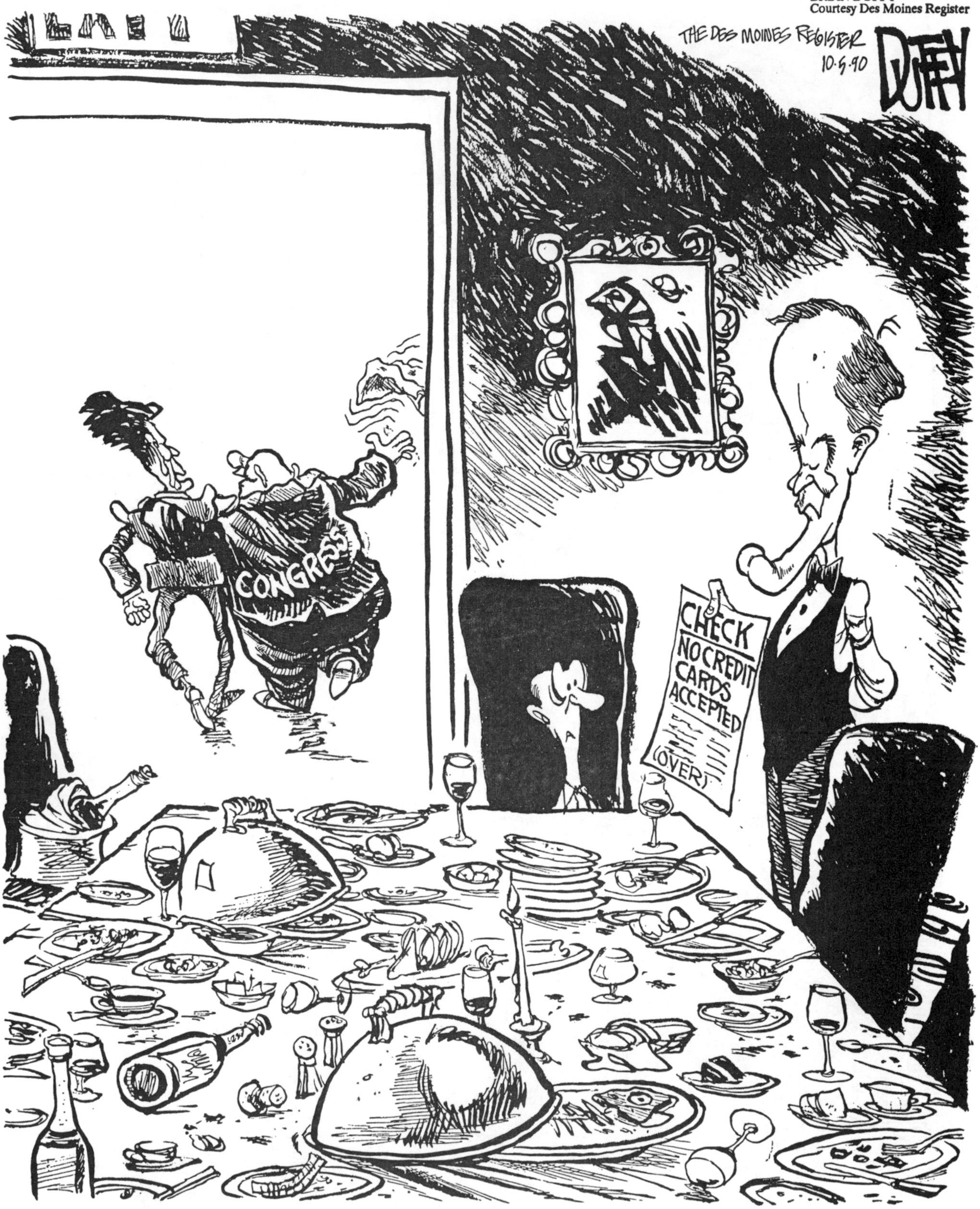
THE DES MOINES REGISTER
10-5-90
DUFFY
CONGRESS
CHECK
NO CREDIT CARDS ACCEPTED
(OVER)

The Economy

The U.S. economy turned downward in mid-1990 as unemployment rose and personal income growth slowed. Compounding the problem was Iraq's August invasion of Kuwait, which immediately drove oil prices higher. Middle-class America was clearly facing hard times.

In late July, the U.S. Department of Commerce released statistics which indicated that sluggishness in the economy actually began in March of 1989. This strongly suggested that a recession was nearer than many economists had been predicting, and before the year's end even the Bush Administration did not dispute that a recession had indeed arrived.

By late September, the oil price jump and continued rising prices in the service area pushed up the consumer price index to 6.2 percent for the previous twelve-month period.

Business responded to the slowdown by laying off employees, trimming costs, and cutting back on production. The nation's trade deficit had been held fairly well in check until the August invasion of Kuwait, but it appeared that when final figures were in the shortfall would be at least as high as the 1989 figure of $109.4 billion.

DOUG MACGREGOR
Courtesy Ft. Myers News-Press

BUBBA FLINT
Courtesy Fort Worth Star-Telegram

MICHAEL THOMPSON
Courtesy State Journal-Register (Ill.)

STEVE MCBRIDE
Courtesy Independence (Kan.) Daily Reporter

GLENN FODEN
Courtesy Columbia Flier (Md.)

CHRIS CURTIS
Courtesy Alexandria Gazette-Packet

STEVE GREENBERG
Courtesy Seattle Post-Intelligencer

DAN FOOTE
Courtesy Dallas Times-Herald

RAY OSRIN
Courtesy Cleveland Plain Dealer

RANDY BISH
Courtesy Greensburg (Pa.) Tribune-Review

DANG – FRESH OUT OF CAVIAR, MR. TRUMP.... MAYBE I CAN INTEREST YOU IN A WEEK-OLD TWINKIE WITH A SPAM GARNISH

PAUL FELL
Courtesy Lincoln Journal

ALAN VITELLO
Courtesy Denver Catholic Register

GILL FOX
Courtesy Fairfield Citizen-News

ETTA HULME
Courtesy Fort Worth Star-Telegram

OUR LARGE NATIONAL INTEREST IN THE PERSIAN GULF

TIM HARTMAN
Courtesy Valley News Dispatch (Pa.)

BRUCE BEATTIE
Courtesy Daytona Beach News-Journal

"They're all at half-staff. The capital-gains tax cut didn't pass."

MARK FEARING
Courtesy Daily Cardinal (Wisc.)

Which international powers can respond quickest to a Middle East crisis?

CHRIS OBRION
Courtesy Potomac News

©1990 POTOMAC NEWS
ASSOCIATED FEATURES OBRION

JOE HOFFECKER
Courtesy Cincinnati Business Courier

HOFFECKER
©1990 CINCINNATI
BUSINESS COURIER

MECHANICAL BULLHEAD

LAMBERT DER
Courtesy Greenville News-Piedmont

MICHAEL THOMPSON
Courtesy State Journal-Register (Ill.)

U.S. Congress

Because the entire U.S. House of Representatives and one-third of the Senate had to spend time with re-election campaigns, quarrelsome lawmakers dawdled with the federal budget for most of the 1990 session. In an attempt to reduce the record $300 billion deficit, they finally came up with a five-year, $500 billion deficit reduction plan on September 30.

The tentative agreement between the Democrat leadership and the Bush Administration came only hours before the Gramm-Rudman-Hollings law would have mandated large, across-the-board spending cuts. The package called for raising taxes on gasoline, cigarettes, alcohol, and airline tickets, while imposing hefty cuts in defense, Medicare, and other entitlement programs. But an unusually obstinate House rejected its leadership and defeated the plan 254-179. On October 6 the U.S. government was forced to shut down all but essential operations in the absence of a new budget. After furious and bitter infighting, a budget was approved on October 27, twenty-three days after the scheduled end of the session.

In 1989, Congress had voted itself a whopping 51 percent pay raise and was scheduled to realize an increase to $125,000 annually in 1990. Strong public opposition forced the lawmakers to back off temporarily. But in August the House and Senate rushed through selected governmental employee raises — including their own. House members now draw $125,000 annually, without honoraria, and senators receive $101,900, with the freedom to accept honoraria.

VIC HARVILLE
Courtesy Arkansas Democrat

ED GAMBLE
Courtesy Florida Times-Union

JEFF KOTERBA
Courtesy Omaha World-Herald

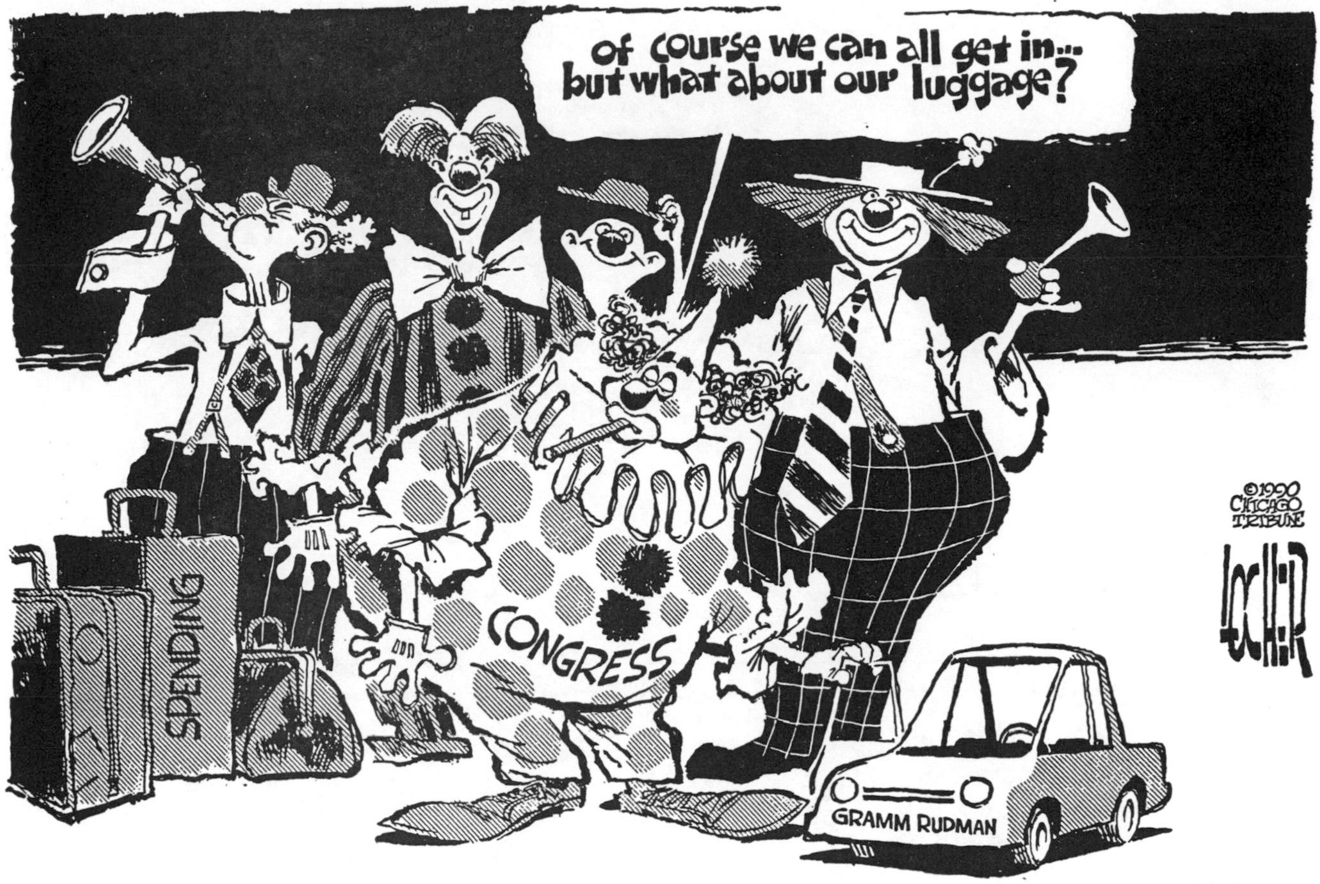
of course we can all get in... but what about our luggage?
SPENDING
CONGRESS
GRAMM RUDMAN
©1990 CHICAGO TRIBUNE
LOCHER

DICK LOCHER
Courtesy Chicago Tribune

GENE BASSET
Courtesy Atlanta Journal

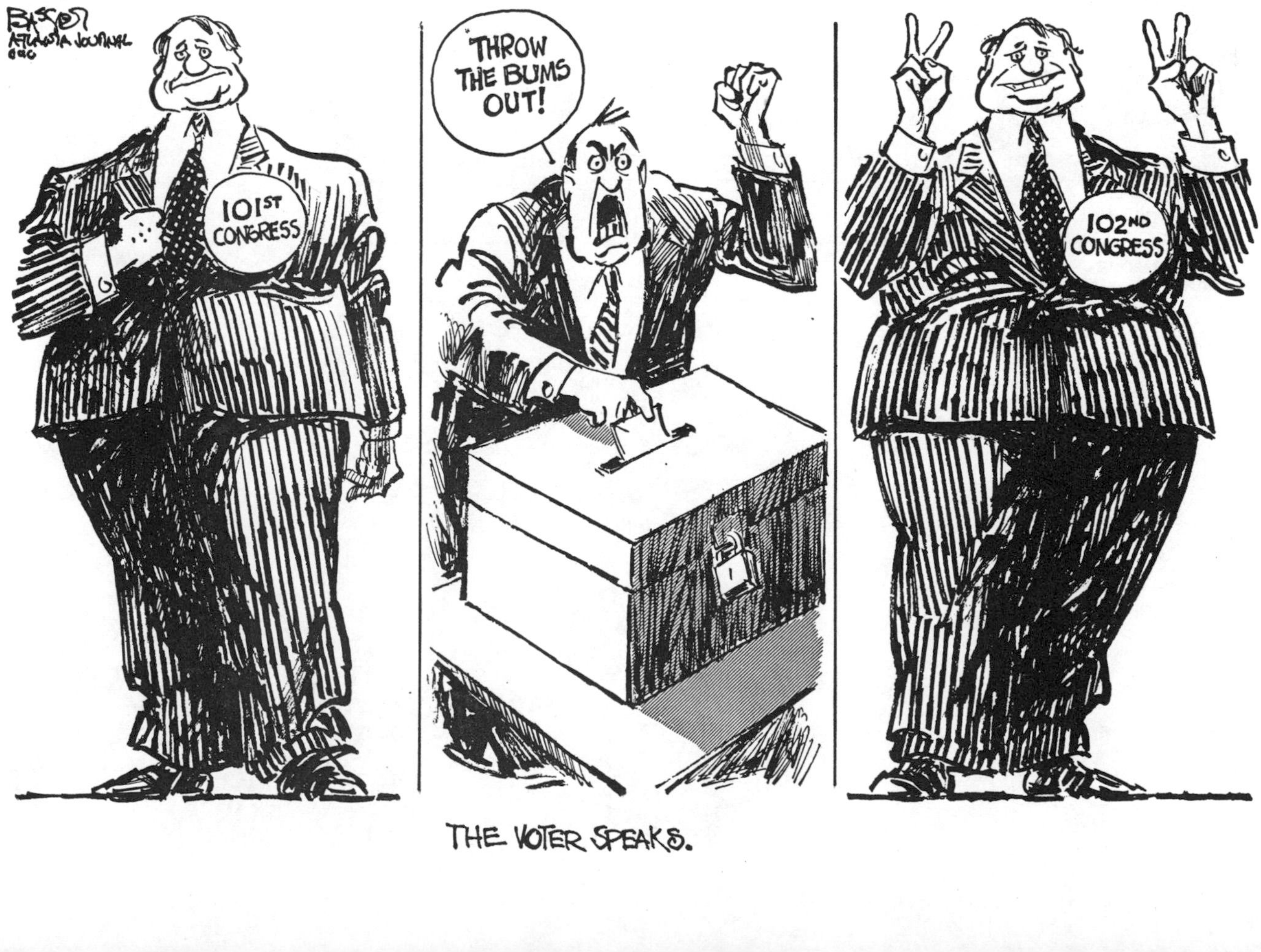
101ST CONGRESS
THROW THE BUMS OUT!
102ND CONGRESS
THE VOTER SPEAKS.

CHARLES WERNER
Courtesy Indianapolis Star

JOHN STAMPONE
Courtesy Salisbury (Md.) Daily Times

DANA SUMMERS
Courtesy Orlando Sentinel

BRUCE TINSLEY
Courtesy Charlottesville Daily Progress

EXTRA NEWSPAPER FEATURES
THE CHATTANOOGA TIMES 11·20·90

BRUCE PLANTE
Courtesy Chattanooga Times

85

HELP!

CLYDE WELLS
Courtesy Augusta Chronicle

MICHAEL RAMIREZ
Courtesy Memphis Commercial Appeal

MIKE LUCKOVICH
Courtesy Atlanta Constitution

STEVE KELLEY
Courtesy San Diego Union

CHAS FAGAN
Courtesy Key D.C.

KEY VOTES AT
THE BUDGET SUMMIT

JACK MCLEOD
Courtesy Army Times

BOB SHINGLETON
Courtesy Southbury Republican-American

THE BUDGET DONE, "OUR" LEGISLATORS BREAK FOR HOME.

STEVE MCBRIDE
Courtesy Independence (Kan.) Daily Reporter

NO MARGE! I think He wants EVERYTHING!"

HANK WILSON
Courtesy Baton Rouge State-Times

Summits with congress are silly -- we all know what's always up there

"OH, FOR GOODNESS SAKE, CONGRESSMAN...IT'S ONLY TRICK-OR-TREAT!"

U.S. Defense

Because the U.S. armed services are now open to women, the call-up of reservists as a result of the crisis in the Persian Gulf presented special problems. Seeing American women military personnel working and living side by side with military men shocked the host Saudi Arabian people–and created a measure of hostility. Traditional Islamic culture had not prepared the Saudis for women in the military, and their view of women generally is at best quaint by American standards. On arriving in Saudi Arabia, female military personnel learned they were required to dress with care, wear clothing that covered their arms and legs, and could not drive a vehicle outside of military areas in order to avoid offending the Saudis.

In November, the U.S. Supreme Court ruled that an avowed homosexual who had been drafted in 1967 be allowed to reenlist in the U.S. Army. He had been forced out of the military in 1984. Also, the Army and Navy decided not to try to force three homosexuals who were denied commissions to repay the cost of their ROTC college scholarships.

Forty-six years after the fact, the U.S. formally apologized for the internment of thousands of Japanese-Americans during World War II, and Congress voted to give survivors $20,000 each in compensation for their treatment after the Japanese attack on Pearl Harbor. In World War II, there was widespread fear that citizens of Japanese ancestry might attempt to sabotage the U.S. war effort.

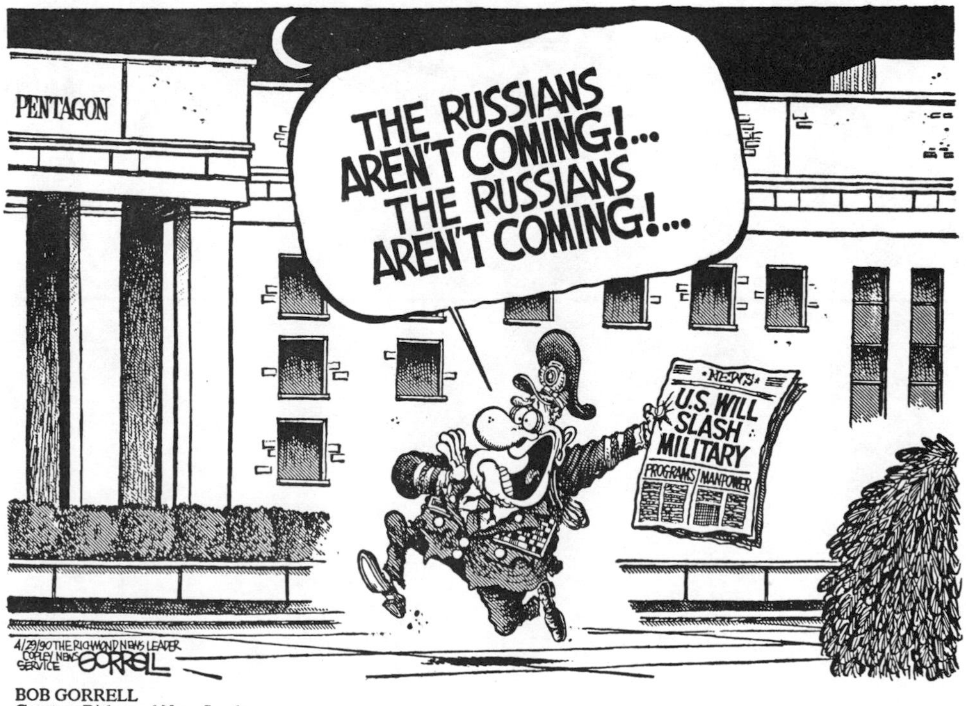
PENTAGON
THE RUSSIANS AREN'T COMING!... THE RUSSIANS AREN'T COMING!...
NEWS
U.S. WILL SLASH MILITARY
PROGRAMS
MANPOWER
4/29/90 THE RICHMOND NEWS LEADER COPLEY NEWS SERVICE GORRELL

BOB GORRELL
Courtesy Richmond News-Leader

DRAPER HILL
Courtesy Detroit News

Coming clean

DENNIS RENAULT
Courtesy Sacramento Bee

CRAIG TERRY
Courtesy Northwest Florida Daily News

MIKE KEEFE
Courtesy Denver Post

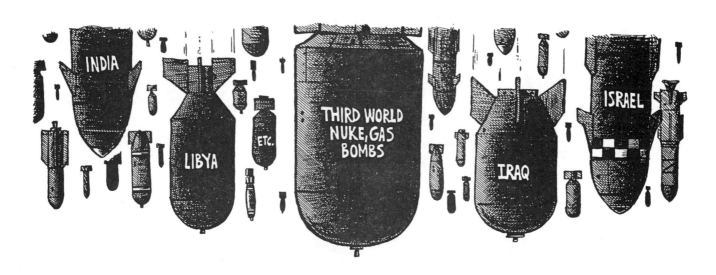

LAMBERT DER
Courtesy Greenville News-Piedmont

The Supreme Court

U.S. Supreme Court Justice William J. Brennan, Jr., a leading voice of liberalism, retired in 1990 after more than thirty years on the nation's highest court. President George Bush nominated to fill the vacancy David Souter, an obscure jurist from New Hampshire.

Souter was immediately dubbed "the stealth nominee" by the press because he was so difficult to pinpoint on the political radarscope. Liberals, realizing that Souter must be a conservative and therefore would give the court a definite tilt to the right, sought diligently to elicit his views on a wide range of issues, particularly his stand on abortion. They were unsuccessful in learning how he would vote on abortion cases that might come before the court, and he eventually was confirmed.

Throughout 1990 the court continued to tiptoe around the issue of abortion and Roe *v.* Wade.

The court ruled that the First Amendment protects anyone who burns or otherwise desecrates the American flag. The decision was unpopular among a great many Americans, and Congress talked of a new amendment to the Constitution forbidding flag desecration. But the idea failed to get off the ground.

ROB ROGERS
Courtesy Pittsburgh Press

DANA SUMMERS
Courtesy Orlando Sentinel

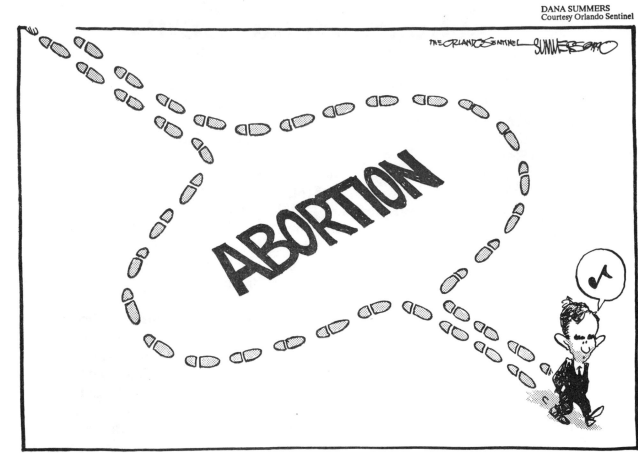

ED GAMBLE
Courtesy Florida Times-Union

JIM MCCLOSKEY
Courtesy Staunton Daily News-Leader (Va.)

WE FOUGHT AND DIED UNDER THE FLAG TO GIVE HIM THE FREEDOM TO BURN IT.

FIGHTING FIRE WITH FIRE

CHRIS CURTIS
Courtesy Potomac Almanac

S. C. RAWLS
Courtesy NEA

JOHN SPENCER
Courtesy Philadelphia Business Journal

J. D. CROWE
Courtesy San Diego Tribune

"...AND THEN,... THERE WERE THREE!!"

PAUL SZEP
Courtesy Boston Globe

JEFF MACNELLY
Courtesy Chicago Tribune

MIKE KEEFE
Courtesy Denver Post

Politics

The voters of Arizona in 1990 rejected a proposal to designate Martin Luther King's birthday as a state holiday, setting off a storm of protests across the nation. The National Football League moved the scheduled 1993 Super Bowl from Phoenix because of the failed vote, and the University of Virginia withdrew from the state's Fiesta Bowl.

In Louisiana, David Duke, a former leader of the Ku Klux Klan, gained 44 percent of the vote in his campaign for the U.S. Senate, despite official condemnation from his own Republican party.

The Gramm-Rudman-Hollings Act mandating severe across-the-board spending cuts in the federal budget was sidestepped in October when a controversial tax package was finally passed in Congress. President Bush, who had been elected on a pledge of "no new taxes," capitulated, approving an alternative minimum tax increase from 21 percent to 24 percent and raising the top income tax bracket from 28 percent to 31 percent.

Five U.S. senators found themselves embroiled in the massive savings and loan institution debacle. It was alleged that the five had attempted to pressure regulators to show favoritism to the failed Silverado Banking, Savings and Loan Association owned by Charles Keating, Jr. Hearings were scheduled by a congressional committee to determine if the five – Alan Cranston of California, Dennis DeConcini and John McCain of Arizona, Donald Riegle of Michigan, and John Glenn of Ohio – had pressured regulators improperly. All five had received substantial campaign contributions from Keating.

STEVE KELLEY
Courtesy San Diego Union

JOHN KNUDSEN
Courtesy The Tidings (Calif.)

JIM DOBBINS
Courtesy N.A.G.E. Reporter

MICHAEL THOMPSON
Courtesy State Journal-Register (Ill.)

ROBERT ARIAIL
Courtesy Columbia State (S.C.)

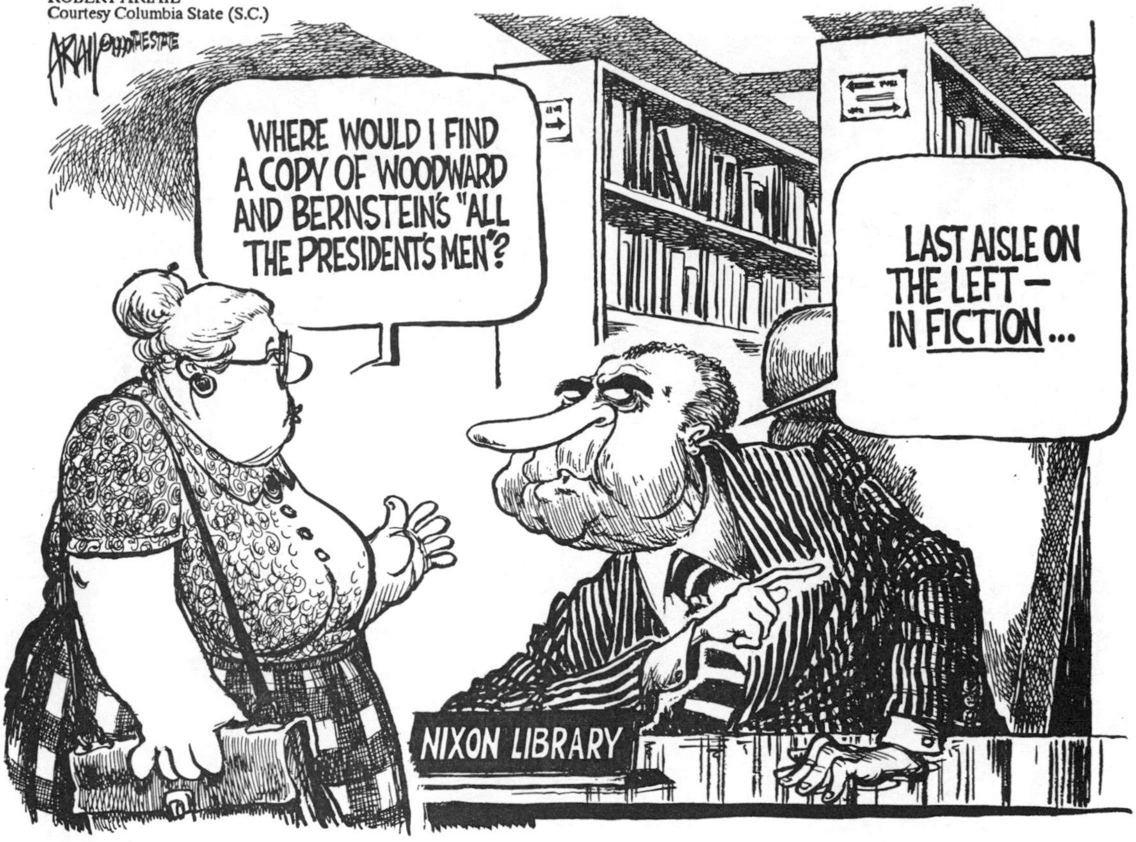
WHERE WOULD I FIND A COPY OF WOODWARD AND BERNSTEIN'S "ALL THE PRESIDENT'S MEN"?
LAST AISLE ON THE LEFT — IN FICTION...
NIXON LIBRARY

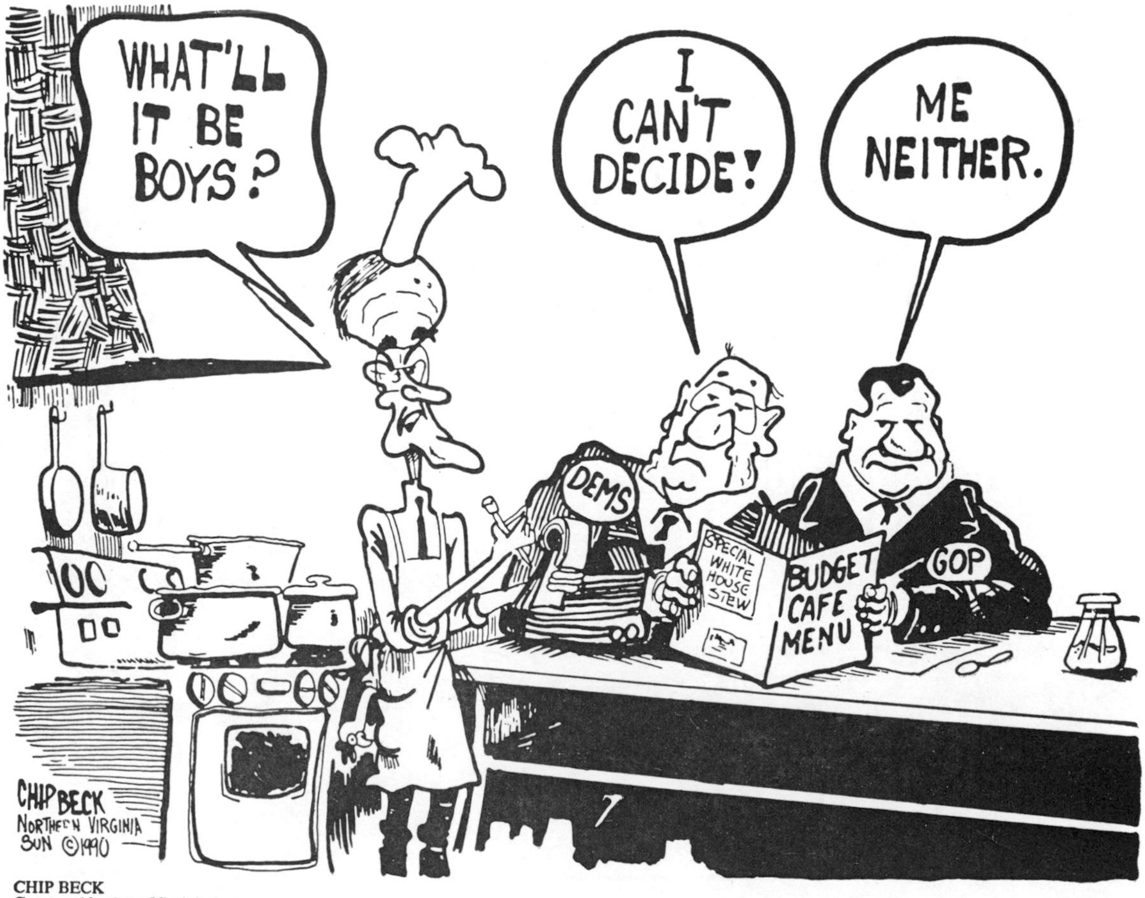
WHAT'LL IT BE BOYS?
I CAN'T DECIDE!
ME NEITHER.
DEMS
GOP
SPECIAL WHITE HOUSE STEW
BUDGET CAFE MENU
CHIP BECK NORTHERN VIRGINIA SUN ©1990

CHIP BECK
Courtesy Northern Virginia Sun

JEFF DANZIGER
Courtesy Christian Science Monitor

JAY CARR
Courtesy Alexandria Daily Town Talk (La.)

FRED MULHEARN
Courtesy Baton Rouge Morning Advocate

CHAS FAGAN
Courtesy Key D.C.

JACK MCLEOD
Courtesy Navy Times

JERRY LEFLER
Courtesy Ventura County Star-Free Press

Pillars of the Senate

CHARLES BISSELL
Courtesy The Tennessean

"GOOD HEAVENS! I'D EXPECTED THE GOODIES TO LAST FOREVER!"

JOHN KOVALIC
Courtesy Wisconsin State Journal

"WELL, I'M GOING OUT TO VOTE FOR THE CANDIDATE WHO TAKES A STRONG STAND AGAINST POLLUTION. SPECIFICALLY NOISE POLLUTION. SPECIFICALLY POLITICAL COMMERCIALS."

CHUCK AYERS
Courtesy Akron Beacon-Journal

BRUCE PLANTE
Courtesy Chattanooga Times

Budget Deficit

President Bush sent to Congress in January a proposed budget of $1.23 trillion for 1991. The administration claimed the new budget would result in a deficit below the $64 billion mandatory target required by the Gramm-Rudman-Hollings budget-balancing law. As usual, however, the administration proved to be overly optimistic about the health of the economy, and estimates of the deficit kept climbing. In May, the administration and Congress began formal negotiations on the budget.

On September 30, an agreement was announced that would raise taxes by $134 billion over five years and would include deep cuts in defense, Medicare, and other benefit programs. The proposed budget, agreed upon by the administration and Democrat leaders, was rejected by the House of Representatives, largely because of sizeable defections by the president's own party members.

Bickering over the budget continued until late October when the final package was approved. The deficit was expected to be reduced by $43 billion in fiscal year 1991 and $497 billion over the next five years. The tax burden on high-income Americans was raised, with the top income tax rate rising from 28 percent to 31 percent. A tax on gasoline was only half of what had been proposed in the earlier bill, and Medicare cuts were reduced to about two-thirds of what the original package had called for.

JERRY HOLBERT
Courtesy Boston Herald

THE AVERAGE AMERICAN DOES HIS PART UNDER THE NEW BUDGET.

JOHN SPENCER
Courtesy Philadelphia Business Journal

"OH GOSH, SORRY! I WAS AIMING FOR THAT PESKY DEFICIT... HERE, A SWIG OF THIS OUGHT TO FIX YOU RIGHT UP!"

GLENN FODEN
Courtesy Columbia Flier (Md.)

TIMEOUT FOR RELOADING

JIM BORGMAN
Courtesy Cincinnati Enquirer

CHRIS OBRION
Courtesy Potomac News

ROB ROGERS
Courtesy Pittsburgh Press

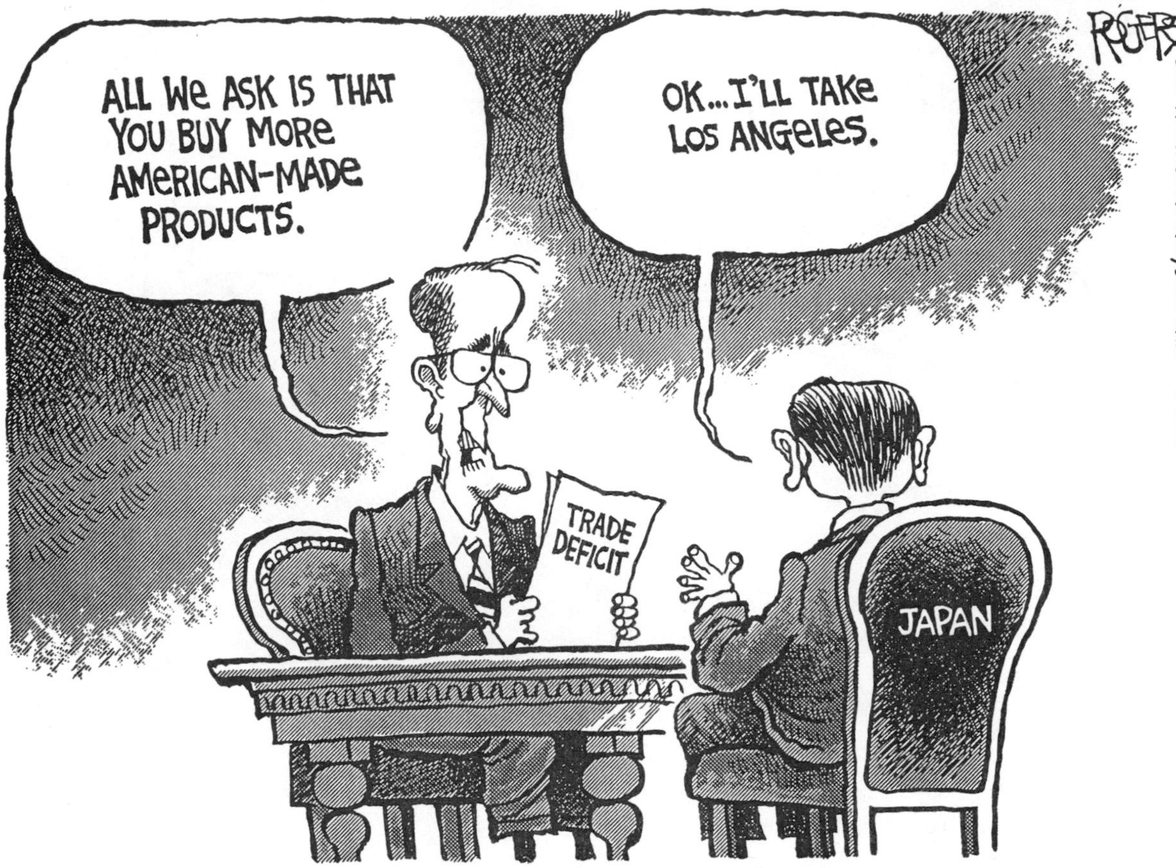
ROGERS
©1990 THE PITTSBURGH PRESS/UNITED FEATURE SYNDICATE
ALL We ASK IS THAT YOU BUY MORe AMeRICAN-MADe PRODUCTS.
OK...I'LL TAKe LOS ANGeLeS.
TRADE DEFICIT
JAPAN

JOHN BRANCH
Courtesy San Antonio Express-News

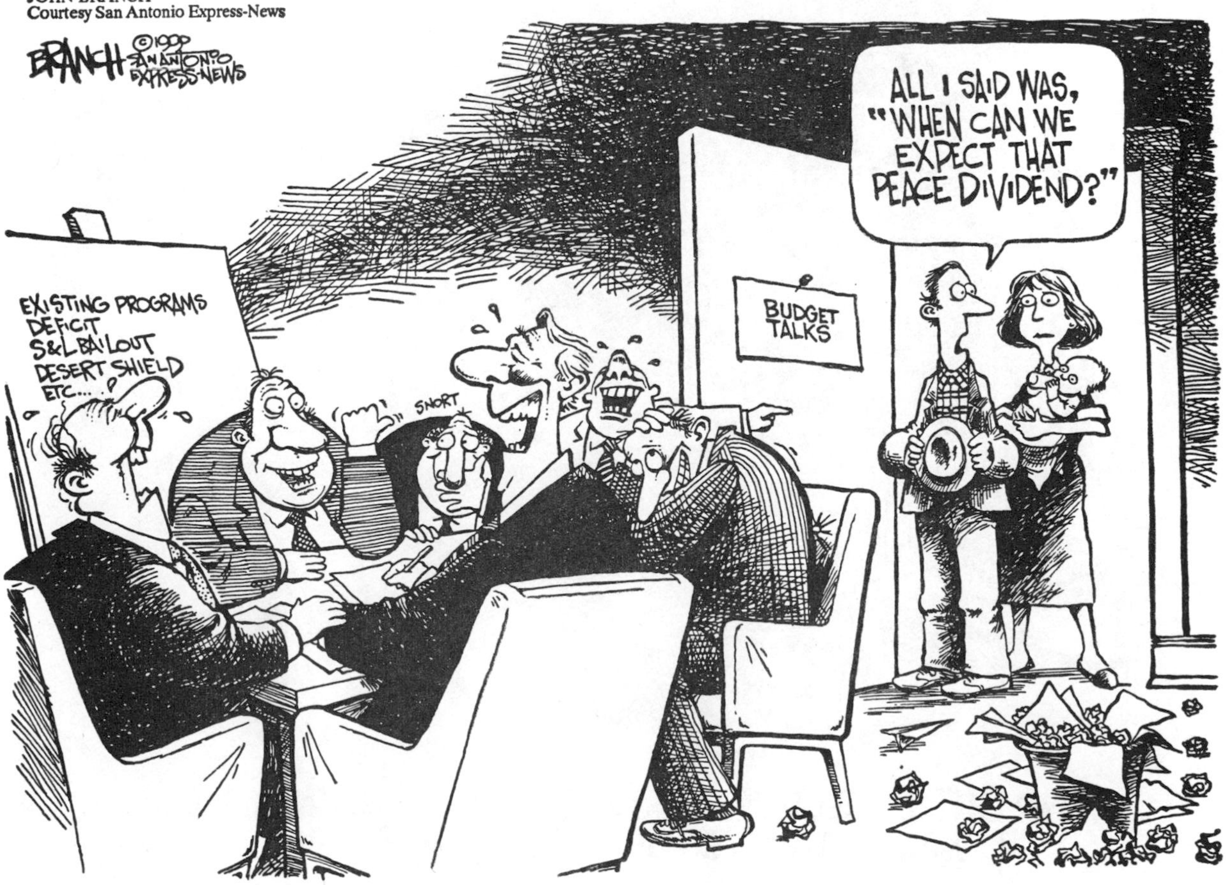
BRANCH ©1990 SAN ANTONIO EXPRESS-NEWS
ALL I SAID WAS, "WHEN CAN WE EXPECT THAT PEACE DIVIDEND?"
EXISTING PROGRAMS
DEFICIT
S&L BAILOUT
DESERT SHIELD
ETC....
SNORT
BUDGET TALKS

Humpty Barry felt accused 'cause he's black,
But Humpty himself may have toked on some crack,
All his advisors and all his campaign men
Couldn't put Humpty's career together again.

PATRICK RICE
Courtesy Jupiter Courier-Journal (Fla.)

GARY PERCY
Courtesy Belleville Journal (Ill.)

...AND OUT OF ELEVEN DRUG CHARGES AGAINST ME,
I WAS CONVICTED OF ONLY **ONE!**

Crime and Drugs

In an eight-week trial, Washington, D.C., Mayor Marion Barry was convicted of a single misdemeanor count of drug possession. It had been a highly publicized and controversial trial resulting from a sting operation in which Barry had been videotaped smoking crack cocaine in a Washington hotel room. The three-term mayor maintained that he had been tricked into using the illegal drug and that he had been targeted because he was black. The jury was unable to agree on twelve additional counts, including three felony counts regarding false statements before a grand jury.

A crime wave maintained momentum across America during the year, and statistics indicated that New York City and Atlanta were the most dangerous cities in the country. In New York, an arson fire in the Bronx killed eighty-seven, a number of children were killed by stray bullets, more than twenty cab drivers were slain on duty, and the subways remained prime targets for criminals. Mayor David Dinkins announced plans to combat the growing menace by hiring an additional 6,000 policemen. Atlanta recorded the most homicides per capita of any city in the U.S.

Courts across the land had large backlogs of criminal cases, and prisons were jammed to capacity. Many states began constructing new prisons while others asked voters to approve money for more jail space.

VIC CANTONE
Courtesy Rothco

WAYNE STAYSKAL
Courtesy Tampa Tribune

BARELY MOVING

JIM DOBBINS
Courtesy N.A.G.E. Reporter

NEWS BRIEF: "BUSH UNCOVERS SUITCASE LEFT BEHIND BY REAGANS"

...and DRUG CZAR Wm. BENNETT HUFFED and HE PUFFED — and RESIGNED.

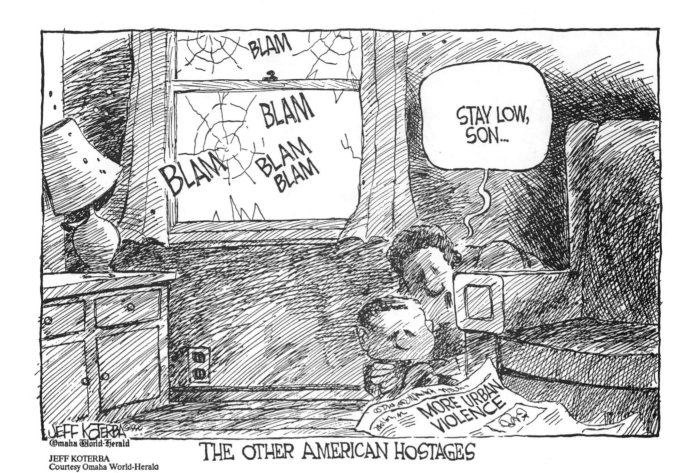

THE OTHER AMERICAN HOSTAGES

JEFF KOTERBA
Courtesy Omaha World-Herald

EDMUND VALTMAN
Courtesy Waterbury Republican

DICK LOCHER
Courtesy Chicago Tribune

JIM MORIN
Courtesy Miami Herald

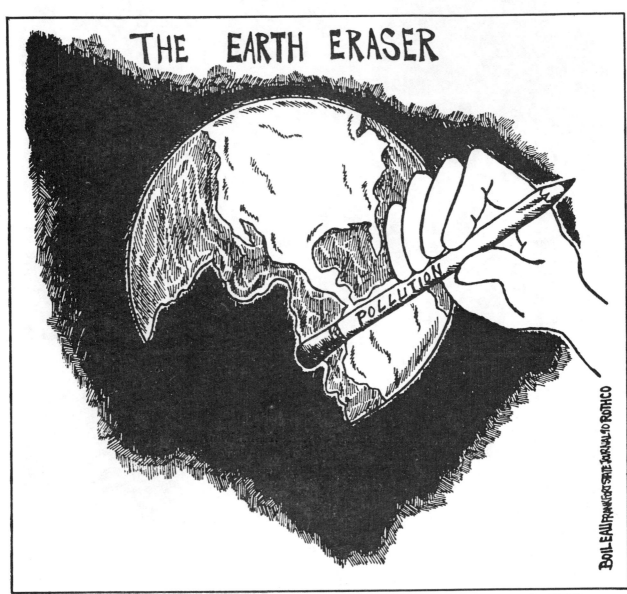

LINDA BOILEAU
Courtesy Frankfort State Journal

The Environment

An estimated 200 million people in 140 countries celebrated Earth Day on April 22, the twentieth anniversary of the event. Thousands of demonstrations, rallies, tree plantings, ecology fairs, and parades emphasizing the need to protect and clean up the environment were staged. Debate continued over whether the greenhouse effect – the trapping of the sun's heat by carbon dioxide and methane gas near the earth's surface – would significantly increase average global temperatures.

Tree-cutting in the Pacific Northwest's old growth forests was said to be threatening the home of the endangered northern spotted owl. Environmentalists rose to the occasion and launched a concerted drive to save the owl. Loggers countered with their own campaign because some 20,000 jobs could be lost if the tree-cutting was prohibited.

Animal rights activists also stepped up their campaign. They picketed fur stores, gained endorsements from celebrities, and distributed tee shirts and bumper stickers in their effort to dissuade people from wearing furs. The fur industry responded with its own drive, asking if it was permissible to kill hogs for breakfast bacon and cattle for steaks. And how about cattle hides used for leather shoes and briefcases?

Recycling caught on as many supermarkets and other businesses joined in a drive to conserve resources. Some scientists, however, cautioned that a "perfect" environment could cost untold billions and was unachievable in any case.

WAYNE STAYSKAL
Courtesy Tampa Tribune

"UH-OH ...THEY'RE LOOKING THIS WAY ... BETTER WOOF A FEW TIMES!"

STEVE ANSUL
Courtesy Wilmington News-Journal

KEVIN SIERS
Courtesy Charlotte Observer

"PO' THING... I TRIED TO SAVE YOU FROM THIS PORNOGRAPHY! JES' AVERT YOUR EYES!"

LEN BORO
Courtesy Phoenix Gazette

JOE HOFFECKER
Courtesy Cincinnati Business Courier

BRIAN DUFFY
Courtesy Des Moines Register

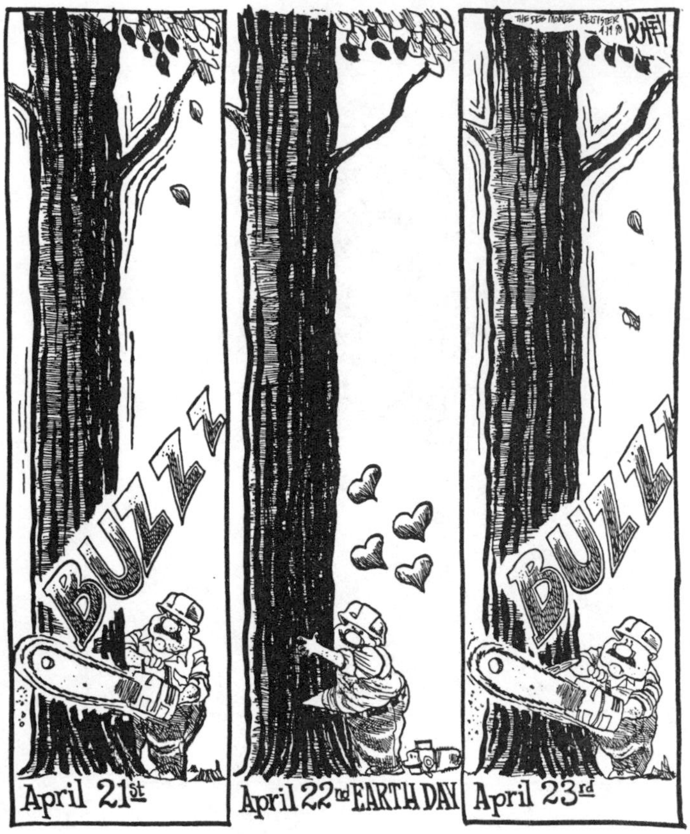
BUZZZ
April 21st
April 22nd EARTH DAY
BUZZZ
April 23rd
DUFFY

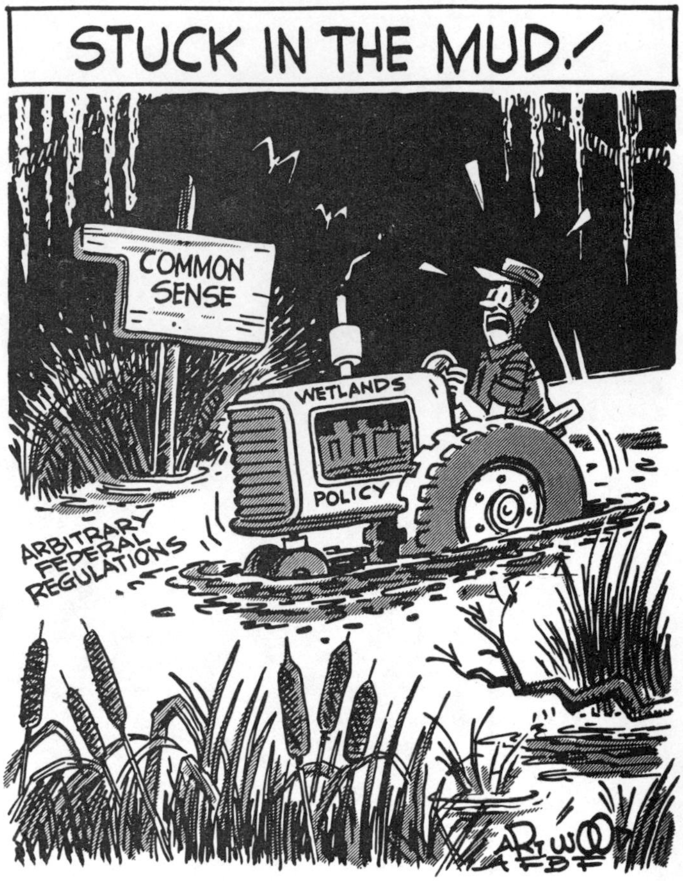
STUCK IN THE MUD!
COMMON SENSE
WETLANDS
POLICY
ARBITRARY FEDERAL REGULATIONS
ART WOOD AFBF

ART WOOD
Courtesy Farm Bureau News

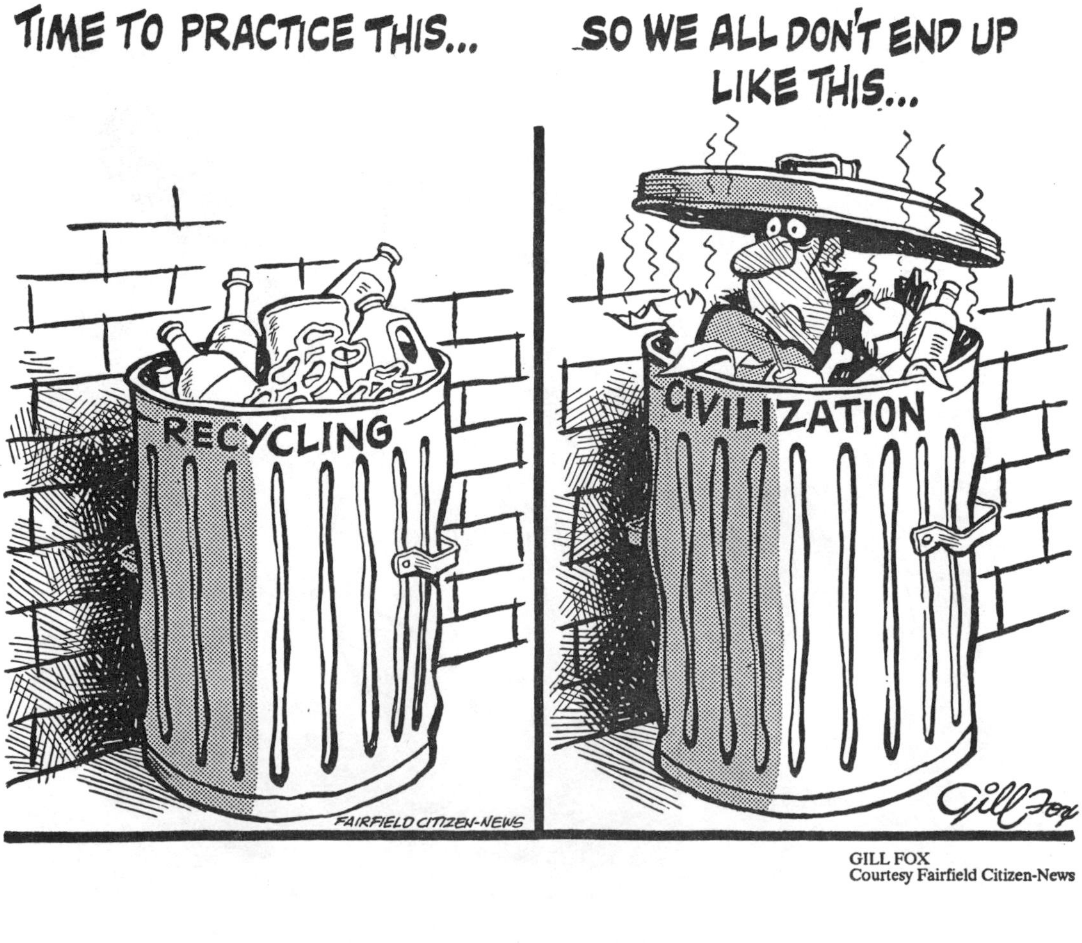
TIME TO PRACTICE THIS...
SO WE ALL DON'T END UP LIKE THIS...
RECYCLING
CIVILIZATION
FAIRFIELD CITIZEN-NEWS
Gill Fox

GILL FOX
Courtesy Fairfield Citizen-News

BEFORE IT WAS TRENDY TO BE SENSITIVE TO OUR ENVIRONMENT THERE WAS ONE GROUP OF AMERICANS...

...WHO BELIEVED THE EARTH WAS A LIVING BEING DESERVING TO BE TREATED WITH CARE AND RESPECT.

WE CALLED THEM SAVAGES

WICKS
© THE SIGNAL 1990

RANDY WICKS
Courtesy The Signal (Calif.)

MATT WUERKER
Courtesy Easy Reader (Calif.)

DRAPER HILL
Courtesy Detroit News

STEVE SCALLION
Courtesy Arkansas Democrat

PAUL FELL
Courtesy Lincoln Journal

MILT PRIGGEE
Courtesy Spokane Spokesman-Review and Chronicle

DON LANDGREN, JR.
Courtesy The Landmark (Mass.)

Man's and dog's best friend

JERRY LEFLER
Courtesy Ventura County Star-Free Press

GARY MARKSTEIN
Courtesy Tribune Newspapers

MIKE LUCKOVICH
Courtesy Atlanta Constitution

CHARLES WERNER
Courtesy Indianapolis Star

DAVID HITCH
Courtesy Worcester Telegram and Gazette

TOM TOLES
Courtesy Buffalo News

Education

Public schools across the country showed little improvement during the year, but educators and policymakers did show a willingness to try new techniques and to attempt reforms. Many policies and practices employed in schools for decades were scrutinized in an attempt to determine if they are adequate to meet the needs of youngsters preparing for a highly technological world.

In his State of the Union address, President Bush announced high educational goals for the year 2000 and declared that he hoped to be known as an "education president." Not much action was forthcoming from the administration, however. The vast majority of high school students tested during the year were judged unable to write a persuasive essay, and for the fifth straight year Scholastic Aptitude Test scores showed no increase.

Crime and drugs remained major problems for many schools, and some large cities employed guards to police schoolgrounds and hallways during school hours and to ensure that all students left at the end of the day.

Schoolground shootings, knifings, and other violence led some schools to have students searched as they entered. Debates were held in many school districts over sex education classes and the dispensing of condoms to students.

The American Civil Liberties Union protested as unconstitutional a prayer at a high school graduation ceremony in Utah, and lawsuits were expected as a result of the ACLU action.

EDMUND VALTMAN
Courtesy Waterbury Republican

"SIR, HOW TO GET TO BURNSTONE COLLEGE?"

JEFF BACON
Courtesy Navy Times

DOUGLAS REGALIA
Courtesy San Ramon Valley Times

KIRK ANDERSON
Courtesy Madison Capital Times

NEIL GRAHAME
Courtesy Spencer Newspapers

MARK CULLUM
Courtesy Birmingham News

This is the education President... This is a school bus...

DAVE GRANLUND
Courtesy Middlesex News

MIKE FURLONG
Courtesy Watertown Press (Mass.)

134

The Census

The 1990 census was marked by apparent foul-ups, charges that the count was inaccurate, and general antagonism from the public. It was the 200th anniversary of the first federal census, and new questions were asked in addition to old ones.

A special effort was made to count the homeless. Some large cities have argued in the past that many homeless families had not been counted, thus lowering the cities' claims for tax dollars from the federal government. Illegal immigrants also are likely to be undercounted since they usually avoid government representatives. Furthermore, young adults living in crowded inner-city areas, especially members of ethnic or racial minorities, historically are difficult to count, as are American Indians because of their mobile life-styles.

About 35 percent of all federal monies are allocated according to population, so city and state governments want to make certain that all citizens are recorded in the census. New York City, for example, had a preliminary count of 7,033,179, more than 300,000 less than the Census Bureau's 1988 estimate and 1 million below the city's 1990 estimate. Several cities threatened to sue the U.S. Commerce Department, which administers the Census Bureau.

DAVID HITCH
Courtesy Worcester Telegram and Gazette

The First American Census of the Homeless

JOHN TREVER
Courtesy Albuquerque Journal

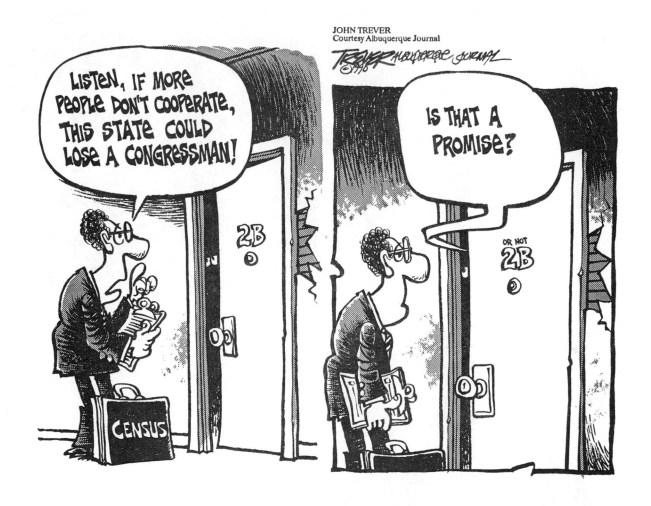

TOM DARCY
Courtesy Newsday

'Include the value of your home, the land it is on, and any other structures on the same property.' — U.S. Census Form

JERRY BUCKLEY
Courtesy Marybeth Cartoons

THANK GOODNESS, YOU CAUGHT US IN TIME. WE WERE JUST LEAVING FOR OUR SUMMER HOME IN KENNEBUNKPORT.

TOM BECK
Courtesy Freeport (Ill.) Journal-Standard

I DEMAND A RECOUNT!

ELECTION RESULTS ALREADY?!

NO, CENSUS RESULTS!

WE COULDN'T HAVE LOST THAT MANY PEOPLE!

VINCE STANIN
Courtesy Daily Messenger (N.Y.)

THERE'S NO PLACE LIKE HOMELESS FOR THE HOLIDAYS

Space/Air Travel

Various types of spacecraft were launched by the National Aeronautics and Space Administration during the year. After a series of successes by the space program, the *Magellan* spacecraft was on its way to the planet Venus and *Galileo* sped toward Jupiter. By midyear, however, technical problems began to develop. In perhaps the most serious foul-up, the Hubble space telescope, launched after a long and costly development program, was discovered to have major defects.

The purpose of the Hubble was to enable scientists to view objects farther away and in greater detail than ever before. But two months after the spacecraft roared into the sky, NASA announced that the telescope could not be perfectly focused. Tests revealed that the flaw was in the main mirror, but a shuttle repair mission to correct the telescope's blurry vision could not be ready until 1993.

Eastern Airlines, plagued for years by economic and labor problems, filed for Chapter 11 bankruptcy, but failed to accomplish a successful reorganization. The airline tried to operate with fewer flights and sold some of its assets to American Airlines, but its days seemed clearly numbered.

All airlines were hit hard financially by the increased price of fuel following Iraq's invasion of Kuwait, and at year's end gasoline was selling for twice its pre-invasion price.

MICHAEL RAMIREZ
Courtesy Memphis Commercial Appeal

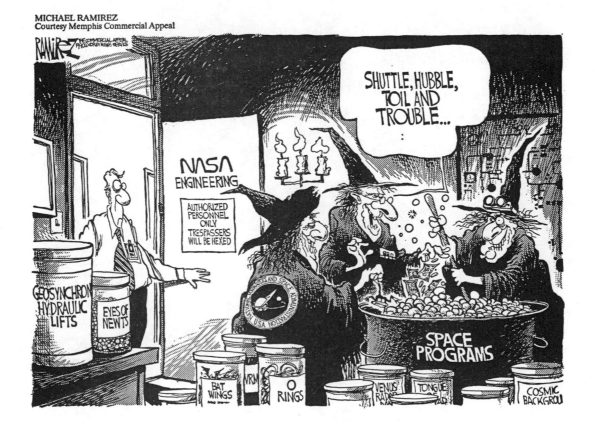

JERRY BARNETT
Courtesy Indianapolis News

KIRK WALTERS
Courtesy Toledo Blade

140

VIC HARVILLE
Courtesy Arkansas Democrat

BOB GORRELL
Courtesy Richmond News-Leader

THE MAN WHO BUILT
THE HUBBLE TELESCOPE:

GARY MARKSTEIN
Courtesy Tribune Newspapers

JOE MAJESKI
Courtesy Sunday Dispatch (Pa.)

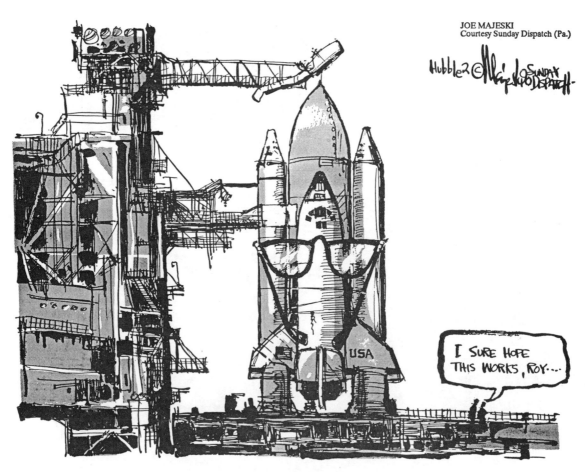

WALT HANDELSMAN
Courtesy New Orleans Times-Picayune

GRAHAM ANTHONY
Courtesy Atlanta Business Chronicle

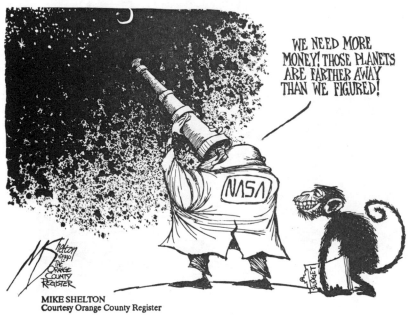

MIKE SHELTON
Courtesy Orange County Register

143

BUBBA FLINT
Courtesy Fort Worth Star-Telegram

DALE STEPHANOS
Courtesy Haverhill Gazette (Mass.)

Pornography

Controversy over publicly funded art continued across the U.S. during the year. Congress directed the National Endowment for the Arts not to fund works of art considered to be obscene. The catalyst was an exhibition of photographs by the late Robert Mapplethorpe depicting sadomasochistic and homoerotic images. As a result, the NEA required grant recipients to sign a statement that no funds would be used in creating so-called art that was deemed obscene by the NEA. Guidelines established in 1973 by the U.S. Supreme Court were to be followed in determining what is obscene.

National attention was focused on a rap music group called 2 Live Crew when three musicians were arrested on obscenity charges. The arrests stemmed from a performance in a Florida nightclub where the group sang songs from their album "As Nasty as They Wanna Be." A federal judge had ruled the album obscene, and a video store owner had been arrested for selling it.

Republican Sen. Jesse Helms of North Carolina was the leader in the anti-obscenity movement, while the American Civil Liberties Union argued that any restrictions stifled freedom of speech.

JIMMY MARGULIES
Courtesy Houston Post

"He says they've all been either confiscated by Jesse Helms, or sold to Japan."

DICK WRIGHT
Courtesy Providence Journal-Bulletin

MICHAEL RAMIREZ
Courtesy Memphis Commercial Appeal

Berry's World

LOOK AT THIS @@#%: POLL. IT CLAIMS THAT 71 @@#%: PERCENT OF @@#%: ADULTS @@#%: SURVEYED FELT THAT @@#%: OBSCENITY IN THE @@#%: ARTS AN' @@#%: ENTERTAINMENT WAS ON THE @@#%: RISE.

NO #%@%!

JIM BERRY
Courtesy NEA

MONA, YOU CAN'T GO IN! THAT'S A WICKED LITTLE SMILE! I BET YOU'RE NOT WEARING ANY UNDERWEAR!

ART GALLERY

CENSORSHIP

LINDA BOILEAU
Courtesy Frankfort State Journal

JOHN SLADE
Courtesy Louisiana Weekly

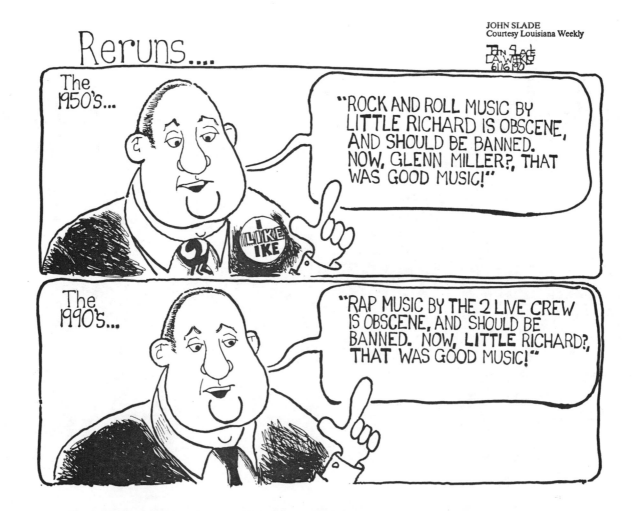

Reruns....

The 1950's...

"ROCK AND ROLL MUSIC BY LITTLE RICHARD IS OBSCENE, AND SHOULD BE BANNED. NOW, GLENN MILLER?, THAT WAS GOOD MUSIC!"

I LIKE IKE

The 1990's...

"RAP MUSIC BY THE 2 LIVE CREW IS OBSCENE, AND SHOULD BE BANNED. NOW, LITTLE RICHARD?, THAT WAS GOOD MUSIC!"

GARY VARVEL
Courtesy Indianapolis News

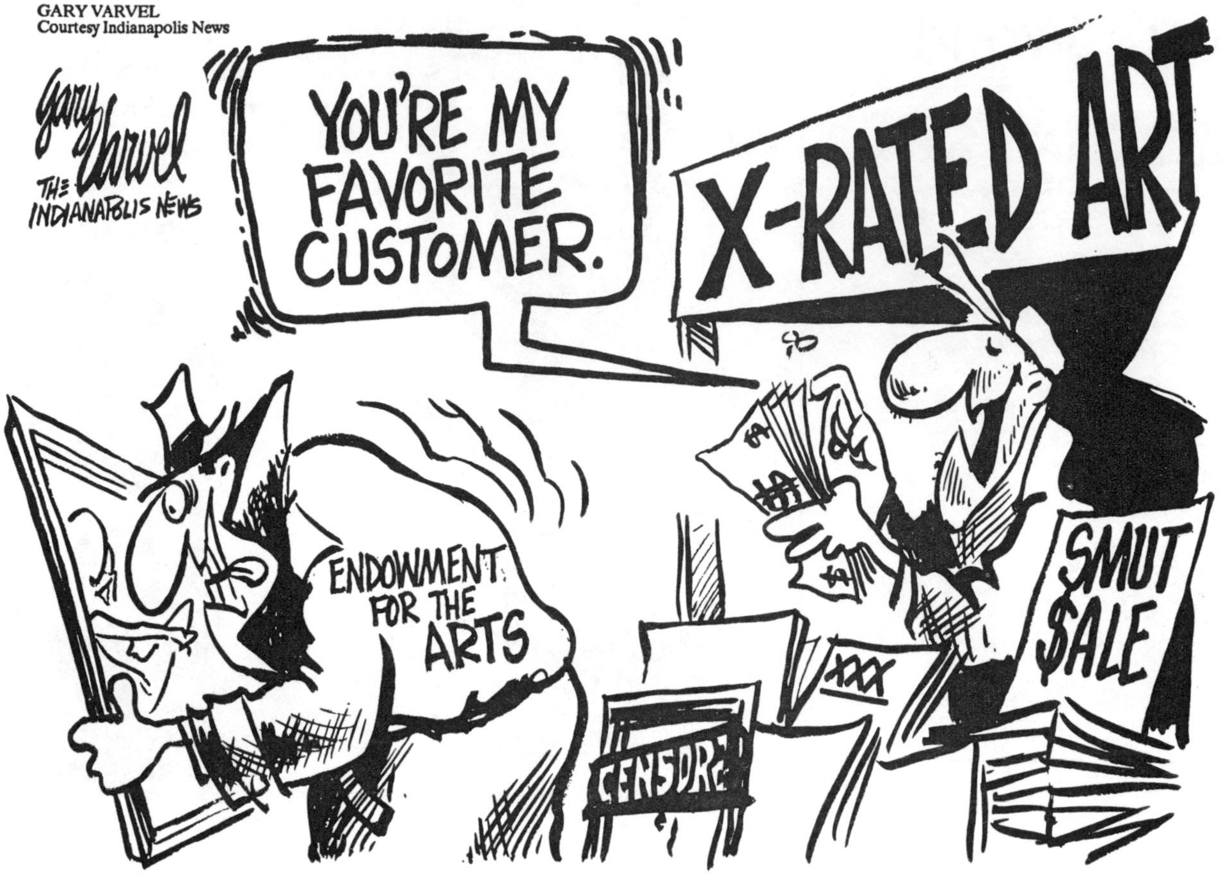
Gary Varvel
THE INDIANAPOLIS NEWS
YOU'RE MY FAVORITE CUSTOMER.
X-RATED ART
ENDOWMENT FOR THE ARTS
SMUT $ALE
XXX
CENSORED

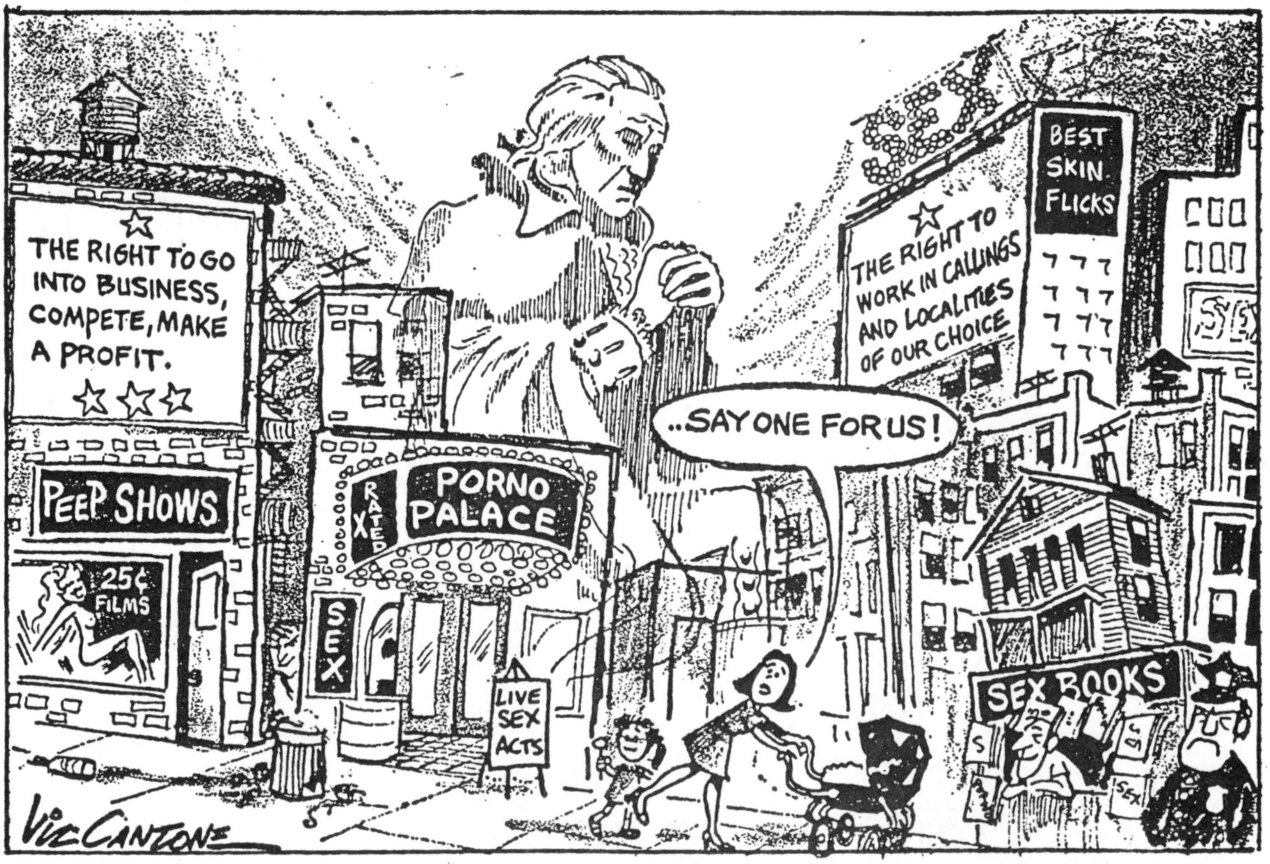
THE RIGHT TO GO INTO BUSINESS, COMPETE, MAKE A PROFIT.
THE RIGHT TO WORK IN CALLINGS AND LOCALITIES OF OUR CHOICE
BEST SKIN FLICKS
SEX
PEEP SHOWS
25¢ FILMS
PORNO PALACE
X RATED
SEX
LIVE SEX ACTS
..SAY ONE FOR US!
SEX BOOKS
VIC CANTONE

VIC CANTONE
Courtesy New York Daily News

MIKE SMITH
Courtesy Las Vegas Sun

"THAT'S RIGHT, LADY! EVER SINCE 2 LIVE CREW AND THE MAPPLETHORPE EXHIBIT WE HAVE BEEN CRACKING DOWN ON ANYTHING THAT MAY BE PORNOGRAPHIC! NOW DROP THAT CAMERA AND PUT YOUR HANDS WHERE I CAN SEE THEM!"

CLAY BENNETT
Courtesy St. Petersburg Times

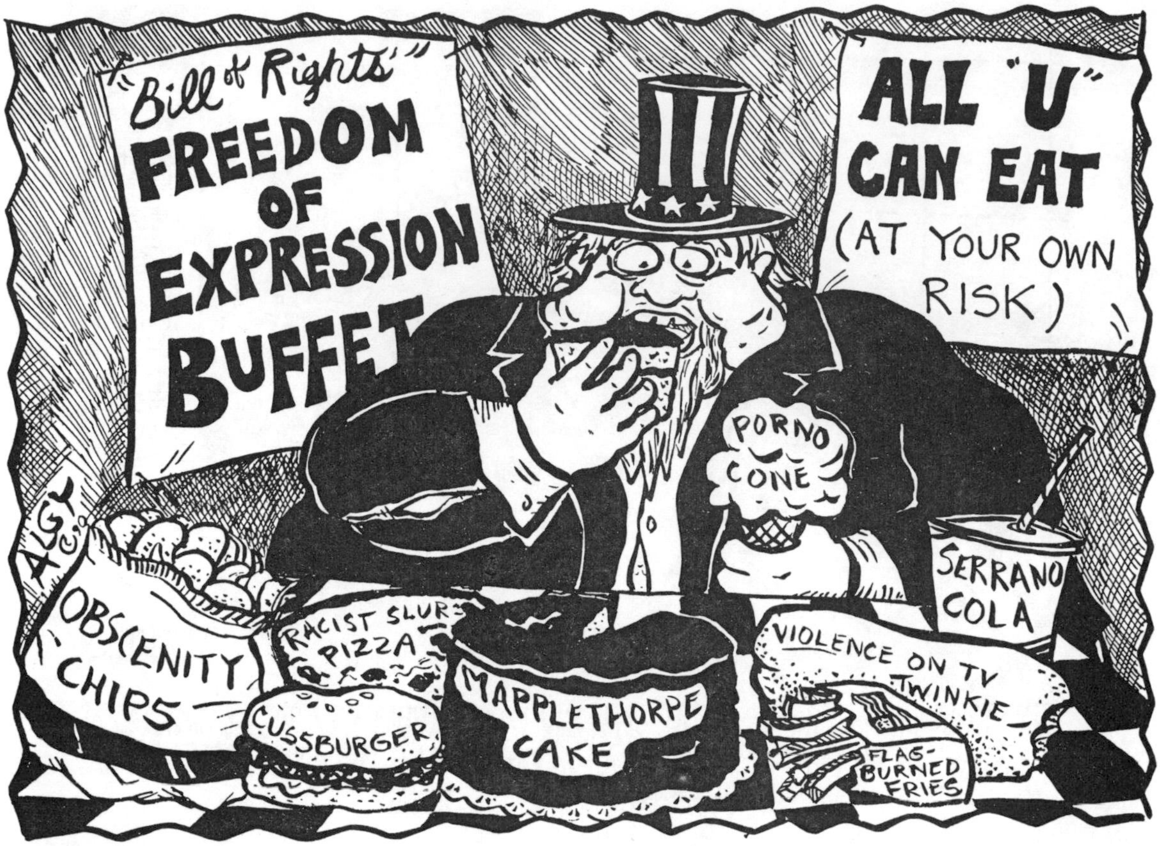
"Bill of Rights"
FREEDOM OF EXPRESSION BUFFET
ALL "U" CAN EAT (AT YOUR OWN RISK)
PORNO CONE
SERRANO COLA
OBSCENITY CHIPS
RACIST SLUR PIZZA
CUSSBURGER
MAPPLETHORPE CAKE
VIOLENCE ON TV TWINKIE
FLAG-BURNED FRIES

LINDA S. GODFREY
Courtesy Walworth County Week (Wisc.)

SCOTT STANTIS
Courtesy Arizona Republic

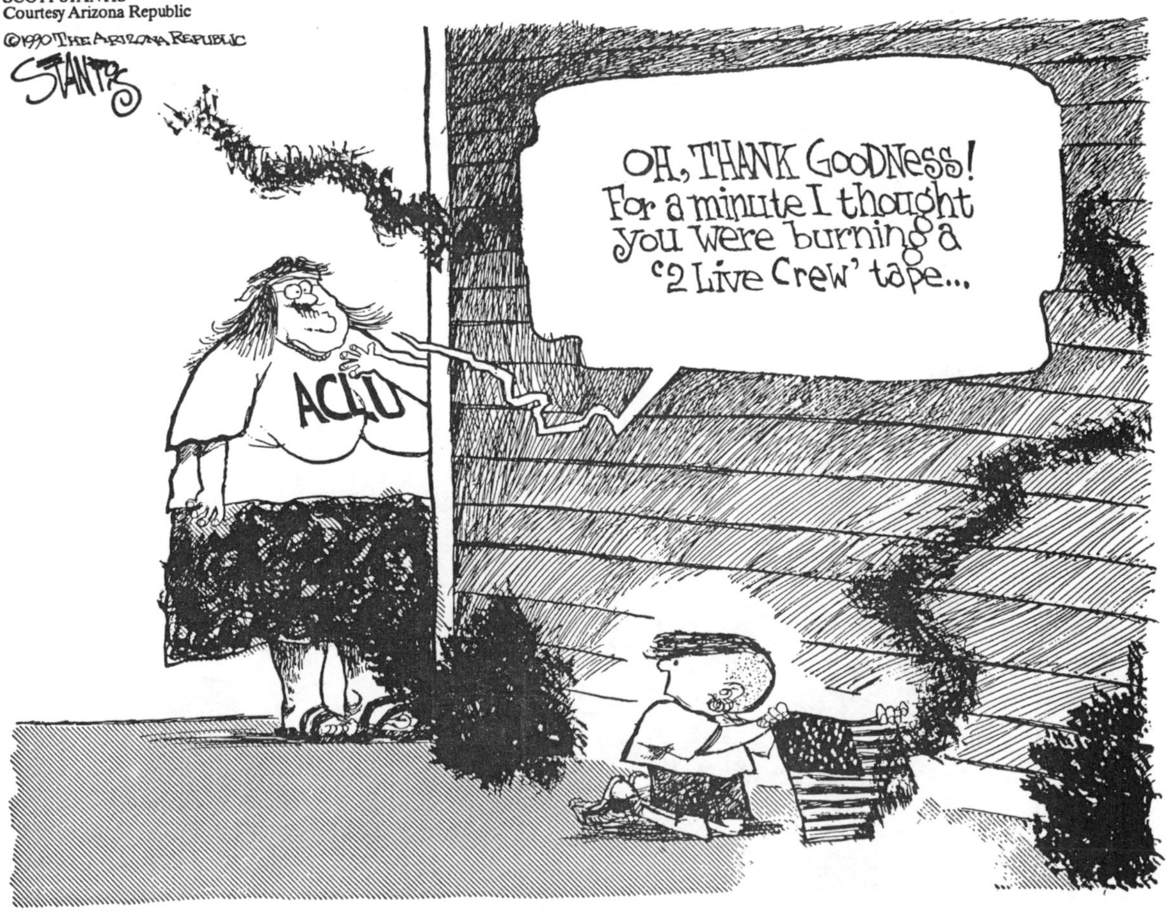
©1990 THE ARIZONA REPUBLIC
STANTIS
OH, THANK GOODNESS! For a minute I thought you were burning a '2 Live Crew' tape...
ACLU

Health

A Supreme Court ruling in 1989 in the case of Webster *v.* Reproductive Health Services opened the door for states to decide whether to limit abortion. During 1990, various laws were passed as states grappled with this controversial issue. In June, the Supreme Court continued to demonstrate deep division over the matter as it issued nine separate opinions in two abortion cases.

The problem of AIDS spread further during the year, with an estimated eight to ten million carriers of HIV, the virus that causes AIDS, worldwide. An estimated 700,000 persons were suffering from AIDS, and the spread of the fatal disease was not expected to slacken for decades. Half of the HIV carriers live in Africa. In the U.S., 154,917 persons had been identified as AIDS patients, of which 95,774 had died. Canada released figures showing 4,455 cases, with 2,595 recorded deaths from the disease.

Improved nutrition and sanitation, along with a big jump in technology, have made it possible for residents of the U.S. to live longer and stay healthier than ever before. But the result has been soaring health care costs, which in 1990 totaled more than $600 billion, larger than the entire budgets of Canada or Mexico. Because Americans demand the best in health care, the upward spiral in costs is expected to continue.

JERRY BARNETT
Courtesy Indianapolis News

ED FISCHER
Courtesy Rochester Post-Bulletin

MARK CULLUM
Courtesy Birmingham News

 Those protesters demanding more AIDS funds won't get any sympathy from me.

 First off, AIDS results from behavior which is entirely preventable...

 And second, cancer still claims more lives.

MARGULIES ©1990 HOUSTON POST

JIMMY MARGULIES
Courtesy Houston Post

JOHN BRANCH
Courtesy San Antonio Express-News

153

MILT PRIGGEE
Courtesy Spokane Spokesman-Review and Chronicle

WAYNE STAYSKAL
Courtesy Tampa Tribune

"REST EASY NOW. THAT MEDICAL INSURANCE YOU JUST BOUGHT COVERS YOU FULLY... UNLESS, OF COURSE, YOU GET SICK!"

Sports

Baseball Commissioner Fay Vincent banished New York Yankees general managing partner George Steinbrenner from baseball on August 20. Steinbrenner was alleged to have paid $40,000 to a gambler to obtain information that might be damaging to Dave Winfield, a former Yankee player who had feuded with Steinbrenner. Control of the club was turned over to the team's limited partners.

It was a difficult year for Pete Rose, the major leagues' all-time base-hit leader. Rose was sentenced in July to five months in prison for filing false income tax records. Rose, who had played for and managed the Cincinnati Reds, watched the World Series from prison as the Reds swept the championship in four games over the Oakland A's.

In the National Football League, a dispute arose over whether female reporters should be admitted to locker rooms after NFL games. Two players and a head coach were fined as the result of incidents, and a court ruled that females have the right to enter locker rooms to interview players.

A dispute between players and owners resulted in a lockout during much of spring training, and baseball's opening day was set back one week. And Roseanne Barr, a rotund sitcom television star, was roundly criticized for a bizarre performance while singing the National Anthem at a San Diego Padres game. She screeched the song, grabbed her crotch, and spit – imitating, she said, baseball players.

James ("Buster") Douglas scored one of the biggest upsets in boxing history when he knocked out Mike Tyson to win the world heavyweight championship.

JOE HOFFECKER
Courtesy Cincinnati Business Courier

PETER WALLACE
Courtesy Boston Herald

P. WALLACE © BOSTON HERALD '90
WE'RE READY TO START THE FIRST EXHIBITION BASE-BALL GAME SINCE THE LOCKOUT, BUT FIRST, THIS....
OH, SAY CAN YOU SEE...

HALL OF FAME
ROSE
HALL OF CORRECTIONS
ALBUQUERQUE JOURNAL

JOHN TREVER
Courtesy Albuquerque Journal

BOB JORGENSEN
Courtesy St. Paul Pioneer Press

JORGENSEN ST. PAUL PIONEER PRESS · 10/90
YOU'RE JUST HERE FOR THE THRILL OF SEEING ME TAKE IT OFF....
PRESS
...ENJOY!

KEVIN SIERS
Courtesy Charlotte Observer

DOUG MACGREGOR
Courtesy Ft. Myers News-Press

STEVE HILL
Courtesy Kansas City Star

Berry's World

FANS

JIM BERRY
Courtesy NEA

MARSHALL RAMSEY
Courtesy UT Daily Beacon

"THAT'S OKAY... PEOPLE USED TO THINK I WAS INVINCIBLE TOO."

JEFF STAHLER
Courtesy Cincinnati Post

BOB JORGENSEN
Courtesy Extra Newspaper Features

M. R. TINGLEY
Courtesy London Free Press

JOSH BEUTEL
Courtesy N. Brunswick Telegraph-Journal

Canadian Affairs

The ruling Progressive Conservative government of Canada suffered a sharp drop in public opinion polls in 1990 as a result of intraparty bickering, increased regionalism, political unrest, and growing pessimism over the economy. Prime Minister Brian Mulroney attempted to placate the restive French-speaking province of Quebec with what became known as the Meech Lake Accord, which would have recognized Quebec as "distinct" in Canadian society. All provinces also would have gained additional powers, including the right to nominate appointments to the Senate and to veto proposed changes in the constitution. The accord failed to gain ratification, however, and antagonism between Quebec and the rest of Canada deepened.

A major gun battle erupted when the town council of Oka, west of Montreal, approved plans to expand a golf course on land claimed by a Mohawk Indian community. The Indians set up a barricade to protest the action and when police attempted to dismantle it shots were fired. After a two-month standoff and numerous acts of sabotage, the army was called in to restore peace. Mulroney promised to settle Indian land claims, update the century-old Indian Act, improve the economic life of Indians, and allow more self-government.

A heated debate centered on whether Sikh mounted police should be allowed to wear turbans.

After eight years of steady growth, Canada seemed to be moving into a recession at the year's end.

EDD ULUSCHAK
Courtesy Miller Services

EDD ULUSCHAK
Courtesy Miller Services

DAVID HORSEY
Courtesy Seattle Post-Intelligencer

©1990 SEATTLE POST-INTELLIGENCER
NORTH AMERICA SYNDICATE

AISLIN
Courtesy Montreal Gazette

EDD ULUSCHAK
Courtesy Miller Services

"Dammit, man -- don't you know there's a recession on?"

M. R. TINGLEY
Courtesy London Free Press

W. A. HOGAN
Courtesy Moncton Times-Transcript (Can.)

JOSH BEUTEL
Courtesy N. Brunswick Telegraph-Journal

...and Other Issues

Nelson Mandela, black leader of the African National Congress in South Africa, was released after twenty-seven years in prison, and former television evangelist Jim Bakker began serving a forty-five-year sentence after being convicted of fraud.

Abortion again was the focus of attention as the U.S. Supreme Court, governors, and state legislators sought to come to grips with the problem. In June, Adm. John Poindexter, national security advisor under Ronald Reagan, was sentenced to six months in jail for lying to Congress in the Iran-Contra affair. Reagan testified in the trial via videotape, but had difficulty remembering any details of the matter.

Wall Street took a tumble when Iraq invaded Kuwait on August 2 and oil prices nearly doubled. Both the stock market and oil price futures fluctuated wildly in the following months in response to the pronouncements of Iraq's Saddam Hussein. Hussein, by the way, acknowledged that Ted Turner's Cable News Network was a major source of his news about events related to the Mideast crisis.

Well-known personalities who died during the year included Pearl Bailey, Leonard Bernstein, Xavier Cugat, Sammy Davis, Jr., Irene Dunne, Douglas Edwards, Malcolm Forbes, Greta Garbo, Rocky Graziano, Rex Harrison, Ava Gardner, Billy Martin, and young AIDS victim Ryan White.

J. R. ROSE
Courtesy Warren Sentinel (Va.)

MIKE KEEFE
Courtesy Denver Post

CHRIS OBRION
Courtesy Potomac News

ED FISCHER
Courtesy Rochester Post-Bulletin

JOE LONG
Courtesy Little Falls (N.Y.) Evening Times

JEFF STAHLER
Courtesy Cincinnati Post

ED GAMBLE
Courtesy Florida Times-Union

STEVE ARTLEY
Courtesy Artley Cartoons

TOM ADDISON
Courtesy Associated Features

RICHARD CROWSON
Courtesy Wichita Eagle

BOB ENGLEHART
Courtesy Hartford Courant

LEONARD BERNSTEIN 1918-1990

TOM BECK
Courtesy Freeport (Ill.) Journal-Standard

HANK McCLURE
Courtesy Lawton Constitution

HANK MCCLURE
Courtesy Lawton Constitution

BILL SANDERS
Courtesy Milwaukee Journal

WILLIAM COSTELLO
Courtesy Lowell Sun

J. D. CROWE
Courtesy San Diego Tribune

"PAINTING THE HEAVENS WITH ELECTRIC BLUES"
STEVIE RAY VAUGHAN 1954-1990

M. G. LORD
Courtesy Newsday

Past Award Winners

NATIONAL SOCIETY OF PROFESSIONAL JOURNALISTS AWARD
(Formerly Sigma Delta Chi Award)

1942 – Jacob Burck, Chicago Times
1943 – Charles Werner, Chicago Sun
1944 – Henry Barrow, Associated Press
1945 – Reuben L. Goldberg, New York Sun
1946 – Dorman H. Smith, NEA
1947 – Bruce Russell, Los Angeles Times
1948 – Herbert Block, Washington Post
1949 – Herbert Block, Washington Post
1950 – Bruce Russell, Los Angeles Times
1951 – Herbert Block, Washington Post, and
     Bruce Russell, Los Angeles Times
1952 – Cecil Jensen, Chicago Daily News
1953 – John Fischetti, NEA
1954 – Calvin Alley, Memphis Commercial Appeal
1955 – John Fischetti, NEA
1956 – Herbert Block, Washington Post
1957 – Scott Long, Minneapolis Tribune
1958 – Clifford H. Baldowski, Atlanta Constitution
1959 – Charles G. Brooks, Birmingham News
1960 – Dan Dowling, New York Herald-Tribune
1961 – Frank Interlandi, Des Moines Register
1962 – Paul Conrad, Denver Post
1963 – William Mauldin, Chicago Sun-Times
1964 – Charles Bissell, Nashville Tennessean
1965 – Roy Justus, Minneapolis Star
1966 – Patrick Oliphant, Denver Post
1967 – Eugene Payne, Charlotte Observer
1968 – Paul Conrad, Los Angeles Times
1969 – William Mauldin, Chicago Sun-Times
1970 – Paul Conrad, Los Angeles Times
1971 – Hugh Haynie, Louisville Courier-Journal
1972 – William Mauldin, Chicago Sun-Times
1973 – Paul Szep, Boston Globe
1974 – Mike Peters, Dayton Daily News
1975 – Tony Auth, Philadelphia Enquirer
1976 – Paul Szep, Boston Globe
1977 – Don Wright, Miami News
1978 – Jim Borgman, Cincinnati Enquirer
1979 – John P. Trever, Albuquerque Journal
1980 – Paul Conrad, Los Angeles Times
1981 – Paul Conrad, Los Angeles Times
1982 – Dick Locher, Chicago Tribune
1983 – Rob Lawlor, Philadelphia Daily News
1984 – Mike Lane, Baltimore Evening Sun
1985 – Doug Marlette, Charlotte Observer
1986 – Mike Keefe, Denver Post
1987 – Paul Conrad, Los Angeles Times
1988 – Jack Higgins, Chicago Sun-Times
1989 – Don Wright, Palm Beach Post

NATIONAL HEADLINERS CLUB AWARD

1938 – C. D. Batchelor, New York Daily News
1939 – John Knott, Dallas News
1940 – Herbert Block, NEA
1941 – Charles H. Sykes, Philadelphia Evening Ledger
1942 – Jerry Doyle, Philadelphia Record
1943 – Vaughn Shoemaker, Chicago Daily News
1944 – Roy Justus, Sioux City Journal
1945 – F. O. Alexander, Philadelphia Bulletin
1946 – Hank Barrow, Associated Press
1947 – Cy Hungerford, Pittsburgh Post-Gazette
1948 – Tom Little, Nashville Tennessean
1949 – Bruce Russell, Los Angeles Times
1950 – Dorman Smith, NEA
1951 – C. G. Werner, Indianapolis Star
1952 – John Fischetti, NEA
1953 – James T. Berryman and
     Gib Crocket, Washington Star
1954 – Scott Long, Minneapolis Tribune
1955 – Leo Thiele, Los Angeles Mirror-News
1956 – John Milt Morris, Associated Press
1957 – Frank Miller, Des Moines Register
1958 – Burris Jenkins, Jr., New York Journal-American
1959 – Karl Hubenthal, Los Angeles Examiner
1960 – Don Hesse, St. Louis Globe-Democrat
1961 – L. D. Warren, Cincinnati Enquirer
1962 – Franklin Morse, Los Angeles Mirror
1963 – Charles Bissell, Nashville Tennessean
1964 – Lou Grant, Oakland Tribune
1965 – Merle R. Tingley, London (Ont.) Free Press
1966 – Hugh Haynie, Louisville Courier-Journal
1967 – Jim Berry, NEA
1968 – Warren King, New York News
1969 – Larry Barton, Toledo Blade
1970 – Bill Crawford, NEA
1971 – Ray Osrin, Cleveland Plain Dealer
1972 – Jacob Burck, Chicago Sun-Times
1973 – Ranan Lurie, New York Times
1974 – Tom Darcy, Newsday
1975 – Bill Sanders, Milwaukee Journal
1976 – No award given
1977 – Paul Szep, Boston Globe
1978 – Dwane Powell, Raleigh News and Observer
1979 – Pat Oliphant, Washington Star
1980 – Don Wright, Miami News
1981 – Bill Garner, Memphis Commercial Appeal
1982 – Mike Peters, Dayton Daily News
1983 – Doug Marlette, Charlotte Observer
1984 – Steve Benson, Arizona Republic
1985 – Bill Day, Detroit Free Press
1986 – Mike Keefe, Denver Post
1987 – Mike Peters, Dayton Daily News
1988 – Doug Marlette, Charlotte Observer
1989 – Walt Handelsman, Scranton Times
1990 – Robert Ariail, The State

PULITZER PRIZE

1922 – Rollin Kirby, New York World
1923 – No award given
1924 – J. N. Darling, New York Herald Tribune
1925 – Rollin Kirby, New York World
1926 – D. R. Fitzpatrick, St. Louis Post-Dispatch
1927 – Nelson Harding, Brooklyn Eagle
1928 – Nelson Harding, Brooklyn Eagle
1929 – Rollin Kirby, New York World
1930 – Charles Macauley, Brooklyn Eagle
1931 – Edmund Duffy, Baltimore Sun
1932 – John T. McCutcheon, Chicago Tribune
1933 – H. M. Talburt, Washington Daily News
1934 – Edmund Duffy, Baltimore Sun
1935 – Ross A. Lewis, Milwaukee Journal
1936 – No award given
1937 – C. D. Batchelor, New York Daily News
1938 – Vaughn Shoemaker, Chicago Daily News
1939 – Charles G. Werner, Daily Oklahoman
1940 – Edmund Duffy, Baltimore Sun
1941 – Jacob Burck, Chicago Times
1942 – Herbert L. Block, NEA
1943 – Jay N. Darling, New York Herald Tribune
1944 – Clifford K. Berryman, Washington Star
1945 – Bill Mauldin, United Features Syndicate
1946 – Bruce Russell, Los Angeles Times
1947 – Vaughn Shoemaker, Chicago Daily News
1948 – Reuben L. ("Rube") Goldberg, New York Sun
1949 – Lute Pease, Newark Evening News
1950 – James T. Berryman, Washington Star
1951 – Reginald W. Manning, Arizona Republic
1952 – Fred L. Packer, New York Mirror
1953 – Edward D. Kuekes, Cleveland Plain Dealer
1954 – Herbert L. Block, Washington Post
1955 – Daniel R. Fitzpatrick, St. Louis Post-Dispatch
1956 – Robert York, Louisville Times
1957 – Tom Little, Nashville Tennessean
1958 – Bruce M. Shanks, Buffalo Evening News
1959 – Bill Mauldin, St. Louis Post-Dispatch
1960 – No award given
1961 – Carey Orr, Chicago Tribune
1962 – Edmund S. Valtman, Hartford Times
1963 – Frank Miller, Des Moines Register
1964 – Paul Conrad, Denver Post
1965 – No award given
1966 – Don Wright, Miami News
1967 – Patrick B. Oliphant, Denver Post
1968 – Eugene Gray Payne, Charlotte Observer
1969 – John Fischetti, Chicago Daily News
1970 – Thomas F. Darcy, Newsday
1971 – Paul Conrad, Los Angeles Times
1972 – Jeffrey K. MacNelly, Richmond News Leader
1973 – No award given
1974 – Paul Szep, Boston Globe
1975 – Garry Trudeau, Universal Press Syndicate
1976 – Tony Auth, Philadelphia Enquirer
1977 – Paul Szep, Boston Globe
1978 – Jeff MacNelly, Richmond News Leader
1979 – Herbert Block, Washington Post

1980 – Don Wright, Miami News
1981 – Mike Peters, Dayton Daily News
1982 – Ben Sargent, Austin American-Statesman
1983 – Dick Locher, Chicago Tribune
1984 – Paul Conrad, Los Angeles Times
1985 – Jeff MacNelly, Chicago Tribune
1986 – Jules Feiffer, Universal Press Syndicate
1987 – Berke Breathed, Washington Post Writers Group
1988 – Doug Marlette, Atlanta Constitution
1989 – Jack Higgins, Chicago Sun-Times
1990 – Tom Toles, Buffalo News

NATIONAL NEWSPAPER AWARD / CANADA

1949 – Jack Boothe, Toronto Globe and Mail
1950 – James G. Reidford, Montreal Star
1951 – Len Norris, Vancouver Sun
1952 – Robert La Palme, Le Devoir, Montreal
1953 – Robert W. Chambers, Halifax Chronicle-Herald
1954 – John Collins, Montreal Gazette
1955 – Merle R. Tingley, London Free Press
1956 – James G. Reidford, Toronto Globe and Mail
1957 – James G. Reidford, Toronto Globe and Mail
1958 – Raoul Hunter, Le Soleil, Quebec
1959 – Duncan Macpherson, Toronto Star
1960 – Duncan Macpherson, Toronto Star
1961 – Ed McNally, Montreal Star
1962 – Duncan Macpherson, Toronto Star
1963 – Jan Kamienski, Winnipeg Tribune
1964 – Ed McNally, Montreal Star
1965 – Duncan Macpherson, Toronto Star
1966 – Robert W. Chambers, Halifax Chronicle-Herald
1967 – Raoul Hunter, Le Soleil, Quebec
1968 – Roy Peterson, Vancouver Sun
1969 – Edward Uluschak, Edmonton Journal
1970 – Duncan Macpherson, Toronto Daily Star
1971 – Yardley Jones, Toronto Star
1972 – Duncan Macpherson, Toronto Star
1973 – John Collins, Montreal Gazette
1974 – Blaine, Hamilton Spectator
1975 – Roy Peterson, Vancouver Sun
1976 – Andy Donato, Toronto Sun
1977 – Terry Mosher, Montreal Gazette
1978 – Terry Mosher, Montreal Gazette
1979 – Edd Uluschak, Edmonton Journal
1980 – Vic Roschkov, Toronto Star
1981 – Tom Innes, Calgary Herald
1982 – Blaine, Hamilton Spectator
1983 – Dale Cummings, Winnipeg Free Press
1984 – Roy Peterson, Vancouver Sun
1985 – Ed Franklin, Toronto Globe and Mail
1986 – Brian Gable, Regina Leader Post
1987 – Raffi Anderian, Ottawa Citizen
1988 – Vance Rodewalt, Calgary Herald
1989 – Cameron Cardow, Regina Leader-Post

Index

INDEX